11th Workshop on Asian Translation 2024 (WAT 2024)

Miami, Florida, USA
16 November 2024

ISBN: 979-8-3313-0855-1

Printed from e-media with permission by:

Curran Associates, Inc.
57 Morehouse Lane
Red Hook, NY 12571

Association for Computational Linguistics
209 N. Eighth Street
Stroudsburg, Pennsylvania 18360

Phone: 1-570-476-8006
Fax: 1-570-476-0860

acl@aclweb.org

Additional copies of this publication are available from:

Curran Associates, Inc.
57 Morehouse Lane
Red Hook, NY 12571 USA
Phone: 845-758-0400
Fax: 845-758-2633
Email: curran@proceedings.com
Web: www.proceedings.com

WAT 2024

The 11th Workshop on Asian Translation

Proceedings of the Workshop

November 16, 2024

The WAT organizers gratefully acknowledge the support from the following sponsors.

Order copies of this and other ACL proceedings from:

Association for Computational Linguistics (ACL)
317 Sidney Baker St. S
Suite 400 - 134
Kerrville, TX 78028
USA
Tel: +1-855-225-1962
acl@aclweb.org

Preface

Many Asian countries are rapidly growing these days and the importance of communicating and exchanging the information with these countries has intensified. To satisfy the demand for communication among these countries, machine translation technology is essential.

Machine translation technology has rapidly evolved recently and it is seeing practical use especially between European languages. However, the translation quality of Asian languages is not that high compared to that of European languages, and machine translation technology for these languages has not reached a stage of proliferation yet. This is not only due to the lack of the language resources for Asian languages but also due to the lack of techniques to correctly transfer the meaning of sentences from/to Asian languages. Consequently, a place for gathering and sharing the resources and knowledge about Asian language translation is necessary to enhance machine translation research for Asian languages.

The Conference on Machine Translation (WMT), the world's largest machine translation conference, mainly targets on European language. The International Workshop on Spoken Language Translation (IWSLT) has spoken language translation tasks for some Asian languages using TED talk data, but there is no task for written language. The Workshop on Asian Translation (WAT) is an open machine translation evaluation campaign focusing on Asian languages. WAT gathers and shares the resources and knowledge of Asian language translation to understand the problems to be solved for the practical use of machine translation technologies among all Asian countries. WAT is unique in that it is an open innovation platform": the test data is fixed and open, so participants can repeat evaluations on the same data and confirm changes in translation accuracy over time. WAT has no deadline for the automatic translation quality evaluation (continuous evaluation), so participants can submit translation results at any time.

Following the success of the previous WAT workshops (WAT2014 - WAT2023), WAT2024 will bring together machine translation researchers and users to try, evaluate, share and discuss brand-new ideas about machine translation. For the 11th WAT, we have MULTIINDIC22MT TASK, ENGLISH-TO-LOWRES MULTIMODAL MT TASK, NON-REPETITIVE TASK, PATENT TASK. This year, the shared tasks were conducted under WMT2024, which was held in the same venue as WAT2024, for the participants' convenience. The system description papers are archived in the WMT2024 proceedings.

In addition to the shared tasks, WAT2024 also features research papers on topics related to machine translation, especially for Asian languages. We received 11 research papers submitted, and the program committee accepted 6 research papers.

We would like to thank all the authors who submitted papers. We express our deepest gratitude to the committee members for their timely reviews. We also thank the EMNLP 2024 organizers for their help with administrative matters.

WAT 2024 Organizers

Organizing Committee

Organizers

Toshiaki Nakazawa, The University of Tokyo, Japan
Isao Goto, Ehime University, Japan
Hidaya Mino, Japan Broadcasting Corporation (NHK), Japan
Kazutaka Kinugawa, Japan Broadcasting Corporation (NHK), Japan
Chenhui Chu, Kyoto University, Japan
Haiyue Song, National Institute of Information and Communications Technology (NICT), Japan
Raj Dabre, National Institute of Information and Communications Technology (NICT), Japan
Shohei Higashiyama, National Institute of Information and Communications Technology (NICT), Japan
Anoop Kunchookuttan, Microsoft AI and Research, India
Shantipriya Parida, Silo AI, Finland
Ondřej Bojar, Charles University, Prague, Czech Republic
Sadao Kurohashi, National Institute of Informatics, Japan
Pushpak Bhattacharyya, Indian Institute of Technology Patna (IITP), India

Technical Collaborators

Luis Fernando D'Haro, Universidad Politécnica de Madrid, Spain
Rafael E. Banchs, Nanyang Technological University, Singapore
Haizhou Li, National University of Singapore, Singapore
Chen Zhang, National University of Singapore, Singapore

Program Committee

Program Committee

Raj Dabre, NICT
Shohei Higashiyama, NICT
Kenji Imamura, NICT
Chao-Hong Liu, Potamu Research Limited
Hideya Mino, NHK
Takashi Ninomiya, Ehime University
Shantipriya Parida, Silo AI
Katsuhito Sudoh, Nara Women's University
Masao Utiyama, NICT
Isao Goto, Ehime University

Panelists

Min Zhang, Soochow University, China
Thepchai Supnithi, National Electronics and Computer Technology Center (NECTEC), Thailand
Kozo Moriguchi, Kawamura International Co., Ltd., Japan

Table of Contents

Program

Saturday, November 16, 2024

09:00 - 09:05	*Welcome*
09:05 - 10:00	*Panel Discussion*: *"Machine Translation of Asian Languages in the LLM Era"*
10:00 - 10:40	*Research Paper I*
	Machine Translation Of Marathi Dialects: A Case Study Of Kadodi Raj Dabre, Mary Dabre and Teresa Pereira
	AI-Tutor: Interactive Learning of Ancient Knowledge from Low-Resource Languages Siddhartha Dalal, Rahul Aditya, Vethavikashini Chithrra Raghuram and Prahlad Koratamaddi
10:40 - 11:10	*Break*
11:10 - 12:10	*Research Paper II*
	An Empirical Study of Multilingual Vocabulary for Neural Machine Translation Models Kenji Imamura and Masao Utiyama
	Are Large Language Models State-of-the-art Quality Estimators for Machine Translation of User-generated Content? Shenbin Qian, Constantin Orasan, Diptesh Kanojia and Félix Do Carmo
	Creative and Context-Aware Translation of East Asian Idioms with GPT-4 Kenan Tang, Peiyang Song, Yao Qin and Xifeng Yan
12:10 - 12:15	*Closing*

Creative and Context-Aware Translation of East Asian Idioms with GPT-4

Kenan Tang[1] *, Peiyang Song[2] *, Yao Qin[1], Xifeng Yan[1]
[1] UC Santa Barbara, [2] California Institute of Technology
kenantang@ucsb.edu, psong@caltech.edu, yaoqin@ucsb.edu, xyan@cs.ucsb.edu

Abstract

As a type of figurative language, an East Asian idiom condenses rich cultural background into only a few characters. Translating such idioms is challenging for human translators, who often resort to choosing a context-aware translation from an existing list of candidates. However, compiling a dictionary of candidate translations demands much time and creativity even for expert translators. To alleviate such burden, we evaluate if GPT-4 can help generate high-quality translations. Based on automatic evaluations of faithfulness and creativity, we first identify Pareto-optimal prompting strategies that can outperform translation engines from Google and DeepL. Then, at a low cost, our context-aware translations can achieve far more high-quality translations per idiom than the human baseline. We open-source all code and data to facilitate further research[1].

1. Idiom 刮目相看
2. Sentences 小明的成绩提高得非常快，让老师和同学们都刮目相看。
3. Context-Aware Translations Xiaoming's grades soared impressively, leaving both teachers and classmates in awe.
Extracted Spans (From Multiple Translations) • leaving both teachers and classmates in awe • taken everyone by surprise • like a phoenix reborn from its ashes • a blazing comet • earned everyone's admiration • with newfound respect • . . .
Human Reference (Sentences Not Available) • treat somebody with increased respect • look at somebody with new eyes • have a completely new appraisal of somebody • regard somebody with special esteem

Table 1: **With our methods, we generate far more context-aware translations than human reference.** The pipeline of our context-aware translation is shown in Steps 1-3. To show results more clearly, we automatically extract the span (continuous words) in the translation that corresponds to the original idiom (Section 3.3). More examples are available in Appendix D.

1 Introduction

Figurative language is a challenge for both linguistic analysis (Dancygier, 2014) and many natural language processing (NLP) tasks (Chakrabarty et al., 2022). One representative task is literary translation (Karpinska and Iyyer, 2023), where the translation of figurative language is one major difficulty. Among figurative language constructs, idioms are especially hard for a machine translation (MT) model due to their non-compositionality. For example, the meaning of the idiom "bite the bullet", deciding to do something difficult, is not simply composed of the meanings of "bite" and "bullet".

Of idioms in all languages, East Asian idioms constitute an interesting subset. Each of these idioms condenses its figurative meaning into a small number of characters, dominantly 4 characters (Chinese: *sizichengyu*, Japanese: *yojijukugo*, Korean: *sajaseong-eo*, all literally meaning "4-character idioms"). As the set of commonly accepted East Asian idioms and their meanings do *not* change largely over time, the challenge of translating such idioms can seemingly be tackled by using a fixed list of literal and figurative candidate translations. This strategy has been commonly adopted by human translators (Tang, 2022) and MT researchers (Li et al., 2024) alike.

However, this approach has a major limitation. The existing East Asian idiom translation datasets provide translations out of context, i.e., idioms were translated without being incorporated into a surrounding sentence or paragraph. Hence, the

[1]https://github.com/kenantang/cjk-idioms-gpt
*Equal contributions.

Proceedings of the Eleventh Workshop on Asian Translation (WAT 2024), pages 1–21
November 16, 2024

translations sometimes require significant rewording to be appropriate in a given context. An example of such limitation is shown in Table 1. Despite that all 4 human reference translations are correct, the first 2 are awkward, as they overexaggerate a teacher's attitude towards a student as "increased respect" or "special esteem", and the last 2 use the active voice that interrupts the flow of the sentence.

In this work, we alleviate this limitation by using a SoTA large language model (LLM), GPT-4, to generate a dataset of context-aware idiom translations. We prompt GPT-4 to use different strategies to translate each idiom within various contexts. Moreover, to avoid accumulating translations by a brute-force and costly repetition of prompting, we select a small subset of Pareto-optimal prompting strategies from a comprehensive set, including zero-shot instructions inspired by human expertise and few-shot prompts that reuse high-quality translations. Table 1 shows the steps that lead to a successful example, where our translations are superior in diversity and quality to the human reference. Our methods also beat commercial translation engines from Google and DeepL (Section 3.2).

2 Method

In this section, we elaborate on the methods and experiment details for each step shown in Table 1.

Step 1: Idioms We obtain idioms from a dictionary for Chinese (Tang, 2022) and online resources for Japanese[2] and Korean[3]. These sources cover commonly used idioms in the 3 East-Asian languages. To test if our method generalizes to uncommon or new words that have an idiom-like structure, we also curate a set of plausible Chinese idioms. Plausible idioms are GPT-4-generated words which are not real idioms, but can fool GPT-4 when we ask it if the word is an idiom (Appendix A.1). For convenience, we use "plausible Chinese" to refer to the language of these idioms for convenience. For the 4 source languages, we limit the target language to English. To our best knowledge, the only human baseline that provides multiple translations for each idiom is the Chinese-English dictionary we use.

Step 2: Generate Sentences To translate an idiom with context awareness, we need to translate a sentence that contains this idiom. Hence, we first generate multiple sentences containing a given idiom with GPT-4. For each of the 4 languages, we randomly sample 50 idioms and generate 10 sentences for each idiom, totalling 500 sentences.

Step 3: Context-Aware Translation Overall, we want multiple translations of each idiom within different contexts. This could be achieved if we only use a standard prompt (BASELINE) to generate one translation per sentence. However, the contextual information is provided not only by the sentence but also by the paragraph that surrounds it. For example, a sentence can be translated more vividly when it appears in an everyday conversation than in a history book, but the BASELINE translation is formal when no instructions are given (Table 2). To always have an option when a context is given, we generate multiple translations of each sentence by the following prompting strategies. Full prompts for each strategy can be found in Appendix B.

Sentence 他们通过威逼利诱，想要我放弃诉讼。
Baseline (History Book) They tried to get me to drop the lawsuit through threats and inducements.
Analogy Creative (Everyday Conversation) They tried to make me drop the lawsuit through a carrot and stick approach.

Table 2: **The same idiom in different contexts (paragraphs) requires different translation strategies, even when the sentence is the same.** The two English sentences are translations of the same Chinese sentence. In all three sentences, the parts corresponding to the idiom is highlighted. Our pipeline is able to offer abundant choices for different contexts (in parentheses) by utilizing a comprehensive set of strategies (in bold).

Creativity is the key to adaptation in different contexts. To invoke creativity naively, we use a two-turn prompt that asks GPT-4 for 5 translations of one sentence (DIVERSITY EXPLICIT) and then for another 5 translations (DIVERSITY DIALOG).

However, we should be able to get context-aware translations more efficiently. Instead of hoping for context-aware translations to be generated by sheer chance, we can directly ask for such translations. To do so, we explicitly ask GPT-4 to translate "creatively" (ZERO-SHOT CREATIVELY).

Furthermore, we can add detailed instructions based on human expertise, instead of letting GPT-4 implicitly choose its translation strategy. Inspired by common translation strategies (Molina and Hurtado Albir, 2002), we use the following prompts: assuming a sentence appears in a paragraph of

[2] https://dictionary.goo.ne.jp/idiom/
[3] https://github.com/LiF-Lee/idioms/

a certain genre (CONTEXT EXPLICIT), using an analogy that is common (ANALOGY NATURAL) or uncommon (ANALOGY CREATIVE), shuffling the order of clauses (SHUFFLE ORDER), rewriting the sentence without an idiom and then translating (TWO-STEP), avoiding using continuous spans (DISCONTINUOUS 1) or multi-word expressions (DISCONTINUOUS 2). For CONTEXT EXPLICIT, we use 4 genres: a news report, a romance novel, an everyday conversation, and a history book.

While we can generate an abundance of translations, many are expected to be mundane or repetitive. Thus, to select a small subset that quickly helps human translators, we need to evaluate all translations to identify the best ones. Due to the low reproducibility and high cost of human evaluation, we instead prompt GPT-3.5 to score each sentence translation on a 1-5 scale based on faithfulness or creativity (Appendix B.7). These two aspects are good proxies for the context-awareness of the idiom translation in the sentence. For each of the two aspects, the final score of a sentence translation is averaged from 5 runs, and the overall score of a prompting strategy is averaged from the scores of translations it produces. We use both aspects to select Pareto-optimal prompting strategies.

After the initial round of evaluation, we reuse high-quality zero-shot translations as examples for few-shot prompting, prioritizing creativity. We choose the most creative translations and randomly sample from them to construct 5-shot prompts. The most creative translations are ones that score a 5 on creativity in at least 1 out of 5 runs. We use a 5-shot prompt with the word "creatively" (FEW-SHOT CREATIVELY) or without (FEW-SHOT). The few-shot translations are evaluated using the same procedure for zero-shot translations.

Overall, we generate 27 translations per sentence with all prompting strategies, totalling 13,500 translations per language (Table 3). After identifying Pareto-optimal strategies, we further apply them to more idioms to expand our dataset (Section 3.3).

For generation, we use the GPT-4 API and GPT-3.5 API from OpenAI[4]. Google[5] and DeepL are used as commercial translation engine baselines.

In Appendix A, we discuss alternative choices of resources, including dictionaries, parallel corpora, evaluation metrics, and LLMs. While we only experiment on the set of resources we choose above,

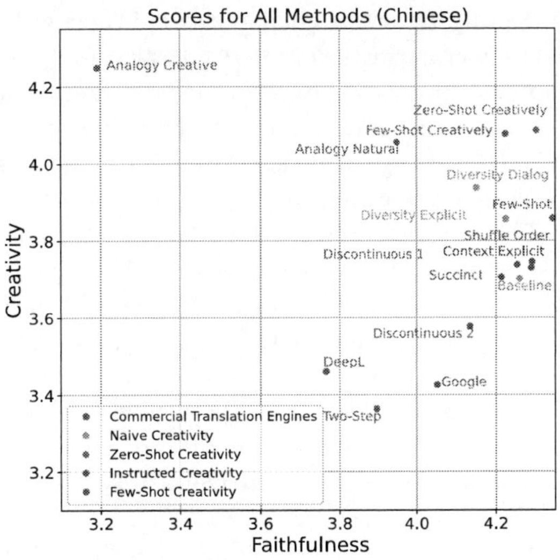

Figure 1: **Our strategies significantly differ in the mean faithfulness and creativity scores.** The strategies closer to the upper-right corner are better.

we already reach the goal of benefiting translators by generating sufficiently high-quality translations.

3 Results and Discussion

In this section, we first analyze the generated translations. Then, we examine how the optimal translation strategies work on a larger set of idioms. We also discuss how the dataset can be extended by an alternative pipeline using paragraph context.

3.1 Quantitative Analysis

To pick the Pareto-optimal translation strategies in each language, we aggregate the faithfulness and creativity scores of the translations from each strategy. The mean scores for Chinese idioms are visualized in Figure 1, while the visualizations for other languages and all numerical results are listed in Appendix E. Here, we summarize 5 trends that generally hold true for all 4 languages.

First, GPT-4 is better at idiom translation than commercial translation engines. Both faithfulness and creativity are higher for GPT-4 translations than for Google and DeepL translations. This ranking aligns with our qualitative observations and supports the validity of our evaluation method.

Secondly, by naively invoking creativity of GPT-4 (DIVERSITY EXPLICIT and DIVERSITY DIALOG), we are able to improve creativity over the BASELINE, at the cost of faithfulness. This result shows an inevitable trade-off between faithfulness and creativity without further instructions.

[4]gpt-4-0125-preview and gpt-3.5-turbo
[5]translating-text-v3

Thirdly, by simply adding the word "creatively" into the prompt (ZERO-SHOT CREATIVELY), we are able to improve over the naive strategy and overcome the trade-off. This result motivates the search for stronger and more cost-efficient prompts, instead of repeatedly using weak prompts.

Fourthly, few strategies based on human expertise result in a Pareto improvement. This suggests that human expertise does not necessarily transfer to strong prompts, at least in the form of short prompts we use to briefly describe human translators' strategy. While a longer prompt with detailed instructions may bring out the full potential of a certain strategy, we do not consider these forms of prompts due to their high cost.

Finally, few-shot prompting strategies (FEW-SHOT CREATIVELY and FEW-SHOT) are often Pareto-optimal. This result reveals the potential in using longer prompts and more sophisticated strategies to improve performance. However, from zero-shot to few-shot, the small improvement in scores costs many more tokens per idiom.

3.2 Qualitative Analysis

We show translation examples in Table 1 and Appendix D. For Chinese, we can compare our translations with the human reference. Thanks to the large number of different translations we get, most of them have not appeared in the dictionary. This shows that our method wins in diversity.

Regarding quality, GPT-4 almost always translate the idiom correctly[6], and the translation quality are comparable to that of the human baseline (Table 1). In contrast, despite producing fluent sentences, Google and DeepL noticably misinterpret some idioms. For example, DeepL mistranslates the Chinese idiom "威逼利诱" (literally "coercion and coaxing") as "bullying" in the sentence in Table 2.

While all GPT-4-based strategies are able to produce faithful and creative translations, the proportions of such translations apparently differ for each strategy. In the GPT-4 translations, we observe two major failure patterns that cause a quality drop. First, GPT-4 fails to follow instructions on the translation strategy, producing idiom translations that are the same as the one from the BASELINE prompt. While this behavior lowers the scores, these outputs are still valid translations, and outputs in undesired formats are rare (Appendix C). Secondly, in the cases where instructions are fully followed, GPT-4 sometimes uses the strategy to improve the translation of other parts of the sentence, but not necessarily of the idiom itself.

[6]We look at more than a total of 10,000 translations by GPT-4 for over 100 random idioms, and we do not see obvious misinterpretation.

Item	Count
Idioms	50
Sentences	$50 \times 10 = 500$
Translations	$50 \times 10 \times 27 = 13500$
Idioms	500
Sentences	$500 \times 10 = 5000$
Translations	$500 \times 10 \times 4 = 20000$

Table 3: **The total number of idiom translations we generated for Chinese.** We first use all 27 translation strategies on 50 idioms. To expand the dataset, we then use 4 Pareto-optimal strategies on another 500 idioms.

3.3 Extension to a Larger Set

To validate our methods on a larger set of idioms, we apply 4 Pareto-optimal strategies (ZERO-SHOT CREATIVELY, ANALOGY CREATIVE, FEW-SHOT, and FEW-SHOT CREATIVELY) on 500 top-frequency Chinese idioms (Appendix A.2). For the two few-shot methods, we reuse the most creative translations of the original 50 Chinese idioms. The numbers of Chinese idiom translations from all experiments are summarized in Table 3.

Table 4 shows that high scores are maintained for the new translations. We would like to further validate our evaluation strategy by comparing against the popular reference-free quality estimation (QE) metric COMETKIWI (Rei et al., 2023)[7]. Interestingly, the COMETKIWI ranking is only consistent with the one given by our faithfulness score, suggesting the limitation of traditional QE metrics when creativity is among the evaluation criteria.

Other than increasing the number of idioms, increasing the number of sentences containing each idiom is also a way to extend the dataset. Though we limit the number of sentences per idiom to 10, we observe that the number of different translations of each idiom keeps increasing with the number of sentences. To show this, we first extract the span in each translation that corresponds to the idiom (Appendix C.7). Then, we use the number of unique unigrams in the spans as a proxy for the number of different translations for each idiom. We count unique unigrams instead of unique spans in order to avoid counting trivially different translations that

[7]https://huggingface.co/Unbabel/wmt23-cometkiwi-da-xxl

Method	Faithfulness	Creativity	COMETKIWI
ZSC	4.27 ± 0.62	4.08 ± 0.36	0.79 ± 0.09
AC	3.01 ± 1.02	$\mathbf{4.27 \pm 0.48}$	0.59 ± 0.14
FS	$\mathbf{4.31 \pm 0.63}$	3.80 ± 0.49	$\mathbf{0.83 \pm 0.08}$
FSC	4.17 ± 0.71	4.07 ± 0.40	0.77 ± 0.12

Table 4: **The scores (mean $\pm$ standard deviation) for the Pareto-optimal translation strategies (denoted by initials) are maintained on a larger set of idioms.** Faithfulness and creativity are in $[1, 5]$. COMETKIWI is in $[0, 1]$. Highest (best) scores are boldfaced. The number of idiom translations from each method is 500 (sampled from 5,000). Faithfulness and COMETKIWI give the same ranking. The strategy AC with the highest creativity is the lowest in faithfulness and COMETKIWI.

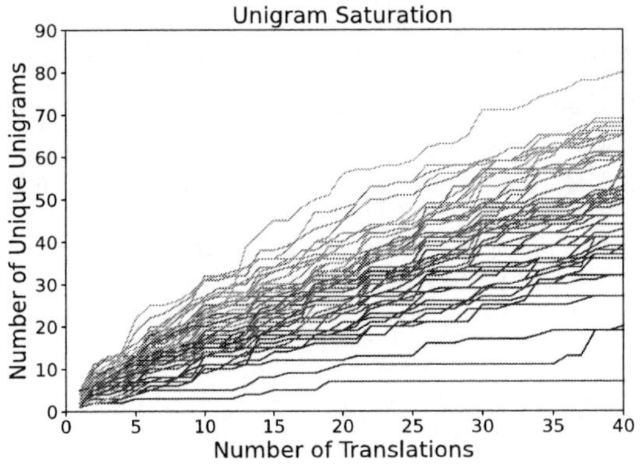

Figure 2: **The number of unique unigrams increases with the number of translations.** Increase rates and saturation points differ across 50 random idioms from 500 top-frequency Chinese idioms. Since there are 10 sentences for each idiom and 4 Pareto-optimal strategies, the total number of translations for each idiom is 40. For most idioms, the increase in the number of unique unigrams does not saturate at 40 translations.

only rearrange parts of other translations. For most idioms, the number of unique unigrams do not saturate as we increase the number of translations (Figure 2). This illustrates the potential of scaling up our methods to more translations (sentences).

3.4 Enhancing Context-Awareness

Contrary to our expectations, we notice that the CONTEXT EXPLICIT prompts often do not change the translation (one failure pattern in Section 3.2). Hence, for this specific strategy, we try to enhance context-awareness with a stronger pipeline. First, we specify different genres and generate multiple paragraphs that contain the sentence. Then, we ask GPT-4 to translate the paragraph, using the following 4 types of prompts. The first type is a baseline translation prompt. The second type encourages GPT-4 to emphasize 3 evaluation aspects, namely faithfulness, creativity, and word choices that match the theme. The third type utilizes step-by-step instructions that are generated by Auto-CoT (Liu et al., 2023). The fourth type is a multi-turn dialog that asks GPT-4 to iteratively improve the translation based on each aspect. The full prompts can be found in Appendix B.5.

For each of the 4 languages, we choose 20 idioms and 1 sentence per idiom. We obtain a total of 800 translated paragraphs using 4 genres and 10 prompts. With the paragraph pipeline, we observe higher variation in translations from different genres than with our previous sentence pipeline. However, the different prompting strategies do not lead to meaningful variations for the same source paragraph (Appendix D.2). Due to the high cost of this pipeline, we leave the investigation of more idioms and prompting strategies as a future work.

4 Related Work

Different from traditional MT models, LLMs can produce diverse and less literal translations (Raunak et al., 2023a). Hence, a series of work has targeted generating diverse translations with LLMs and selecting the best. On one hand, translations can be generated from scratch using various prompting strategies. Then, ensembling methods can be applied to select the best candidates (Farinhas et al., 2023). On the other hand, candidates can be further refined. Some examples include refining candidates generated by other machine translation systems (Raunak et al., 2023b), iterative editing (Chen et al., 2024; Briakou et al., 2024), self-correction (Feng et al., 2024a), and multi-agent debate (Liang et al., 2023). While existing work focused mostly on general translation, our work contributes in the more challenging task of generating diverse, high-quality translations for idioms.

5 Conclusion

In this work, we thoroughly test prompting strategies that generate different translations for an East Asian idiom. We identify the strategies that generate most creative and faithful translations. To our surprise, the prompts derived from human experience do not consistently generate quantitatively better translations. Finally, we use the Pareto optimal strategies to construct a dataset of high quality translations, which can help human translators.

Limitations

Limitations of our work include:

- **No external databases.** We discover that few-shot prompts could produce competitive translations, but are not able to use external translation as examples due to the lack of a high-quality and well-aligned parallel corpora.
- **No multi-agent or role-playing.** These orthogonal prompt-based directions provide effective methods that could possibly be combined with ours.
- **No language-specific strategies.** Our set of translation strategies is language-agnostic and thus not exhaustive.
- **No idiom categorization.** We do not consider the diverse linguistically motivated categorization of idioms in our general pipeline.
- **No expert evaluation.** We are not able to obtain the evaluation of translation quality from a large crowd of full-time professional translators due to cost and resource limits. Opinions from a smaller set of evaluators may carry personal biases, especially for the creative translation task we are investigating. Thus, we do not include human study in this work.

We would like to address these limitations in future work.

References

Sidney Black, Stella Biderman, Eric Hallahan, Quentin Anthony, Leo Gao, Laurence Golding, Horace He, Connor Leahy, Kyle McDonell, Jason Phang, Michael Pieler, Usvsn Sai Prashanth, Shivanshu Purohit, Laria Reynolds, Jonathan Tow, Ben Wang, and Samuel Weinbach. 2022. GPT-NeoX-20B: An open-source autoregressive language model. In *Proceedings of BigScience Episode #5 – Workshop on Challenges & Perspectives in Creating Large Language Models*, pages 95–136, virtual+Dublin. Association for Computational Linguistics.

Eleftheria Briakou, Jiaming Luo, Colin Cherry, and Markus Freitag. 2024. Translating step-by-step: Decomposing the translation process for improved translation quality of long-form texts. *arXiv preprint arXiv:2409.06790*.

Tuhin Chakrabarty, Yejin Choi, and Vered Shwartz. 2022. It's not rocket science: Interpreting figurative language in narratives. *Transactions of the Association for Computational Linguistics*, 10:589–606.

Pinzhen Chen, Zhicheng Guo, Barry Haddow, and Kenneth Heafield. 2024. Iterative translation refinement with large language models. *Preprint*, arXiv:2306.03856.

Hyung Won Chung, Le Hou, Shayne Longpre, Barret Zoph, Yi Tay, William Fedus, Yunxuan Li, Xuezhi Wang, Mostafa Dehghani, Siddhartha Brahma, Albert Webson, Shixiang Shane Gu, Zhuyun Dai, Mirac Suzgun, Xinyun Chen, Aakanksha Chowdhery, Alex Castro-Ros, Marie Pellat, Kevin Robinson, Dasha Valter, Sharan Narang, Gaurav Mishra, Adams Yu, Vincent Zhao, Yanping Huang, Andrew Dai, Hongkun Yu, Slav Petrov, Ed H. Chi, Jeff Dean, Jacob Devlin, Adam Roberts, Denny Zhou, Quoc V. Le, and Jason Wei. 2024. Scaling instruction-finetuned language models. *Journal of Machine Learning Research*, 25(70):1–53.

Barbara Dancygier. 2014. *Figurative language*. Cambridge University Press.

António Farinhas, José de Souza, and Andre Martins. 2023. An empirical study of translation hypothesis ensembling with large language models. In *Proceedings of the 2023 Conference on Empirical Methods in Natural Language Processing*, pages 11956–11970, Singapore. Association for Computational Linguistics.

Yunlong Feng, Yang Xu, Libo Qin, Yasheng Wang, and Wanxiang Che. 2024a. Improving language model reasoning with self-motivated learning. In *Proceedings of the 2024 Joint International Conference on Computational Linguistics, Language Resources and Evaluation (LREC-COLING 2024)*, pages 8840–8852, Torino, Italia. ELRA and ICCL.

Zhaopeng Feng, Yan Zhang, Hao Li, Wenqiang Liu, Jun Lang, Yang Feng, Jian Wu, and Zuozhu Liu. 2024b. Improving llm-based machine translation with systematic self-correction. *Preprint*, arXiv:2402.16379.

Patrick Fernandes, Daniel Deutsch, Mara Finkelstein, Parker Riley, André Martins, Graham Neubig, Ankush Garg, Jonathan Clark, Markus Freitag, and Orhan Firat. 2023. The devil is in the errors: Leveraging large language models for fine-grained machine translation evaluation. In *Proceedings of the Eighth Conference on Machine Translation*, pages 1066–1083, Singapore. Association for Computational Linguistics.

Markus Freitag, George Foster, David Grangier, Viresh Ratnakar, Qijun Tan, and Wolfgang Macherey. 2021. Experts, errors, and context: A large-scale study of human evaluation for machine translation. *Transactions of the Association for Computational Linguistics*, 9:1460–1474.

Zhiwei He, Tian Liang, Wenxiang Jiao, Zhuosheng Zhang, Yujiu Yang, Rui Wang, Zhaopeng Tu, Shuming Shi, and Xing Wang. 2023. Exploring human-like translation strategy with large language models. *Preprint*, arXiv:2305.04118.

Yuchen Jiang, Tianyu Liu, Shuming Ma, Dongdong Zhang, Jian Yang, Haoyang Huang, Rico Sennrich, Ryan Cotterell, Mrinmaya Sachan, and Ming Zhou. 2022. BlonDe: An automatic evaluation metric for document-level machine translation. In *Proceedings of the 2022 Conference of the North American Chapter of the Association for Computational Linguistics: Human Language Technologies*, pages 1550–1565, Seattle, United States. Association for Computational Linguistics.

Wenxiang Jiao, Wenxuan Wang, Jen tse Huang, Xing Wang, Shuming Shi, and Zhaopeng Tu. 2023. Is chatgpt a good translator? yes with gpt-4 as the engine. *Preprint*, arXiv:2301.08745.

Marzena Karpinska and Mohit Iyyer. 2023. Large language models effectively leverage document-level context for literary translation, but critical errors persist. In *Proceedings of the Eighth Conference on Machine Translation*, pages 419–451, Singapore. Association for Computational Linguistics.

Tom Kocmi, Eleftherios Avramidis, Rachel Bawden, Ondřej Bojar, Anton Dvorkovich, Christian Federmann, Mark Fishel, Markus Freitag, Thamme Gowda, Roman Grundkiewicz, Barry Haddow, Philipp Koehn, Benjamin Marie, Christof Monz, Makoto Morishita, Kenton Murray, Makoto Nagata, Toshiaki Nakazawa, Martin Popel, Maja Popović, and Mariya Shmatova. 2023. Findings of the 2023 conference on machine translation (WMT23): LLMs are here but not quite there yet. In *Proceedings of the Eighth Conference on Machine Translation*, pages 1–42, Singapore. Association for Computational Linguistics.

Tom Kocmi and Christian Federmann. 2023. GEMBA-MQM: Detecting translation quality error spans with GPT-4. In *Proceedings of the Eighth Conference on Machine Translation*, pages 768–775, Singapore. Association for Computational Linguistics.

Shuang Li, Jiangjie Chen, Siyu Yuan, Xinyi Wu, Hao Yang, Shimin Tao, and Yanghua Xiao. 2024. Translate meanings, not just words: Idiomkb'Ă'Źs role in optimizing idiomatic translation with language models. In *Proceedings of the AAAI Conference on Artificial Intelligence*, volume 38, pages 18554–18563.

Tian Liang, Zhiwei He, Wenxiang Jiao, Xing Wang, Yan Wang, Rui Wang, Yujiu Yang, Zhaopeng Tu, and Shuming Shi. 2023. Encouraging divergent thinking in large language models through multi-agent debate. *Preprint*, arXiv:2305.19118.

Yang Liu, Dan Iter, Yichong Xu, Shuohang Wang, Ruochen Xu, and Chenguang Zhu. 2023. G-eval: NLG evaluation using gpt-4 with better human alignment. In *Proceedings of the 2023 Conference on Empirical Methods in Natural Language Processing*, pages 2511–2522, Singapore. Association for Computational Linguistics.

Chenyang Lyu, Zefeng Du, Jitao Xu, Yitao Duan, Minghao Wu, Teresa Lynn, Alham Fikri Aji, Derek F. Wong, and Longyue Wang. 2024. A paradigm shift: The future of machine translation lies with large language models. In *Proceedings of the 2024 Joint International Conference on Computational Linguistics, Language Resources and Evaluation (LREC-COLING 2024)*, pages 1339–1352, Torino, Italia. ELRA and ICCL.

Lucía Molina and Amparo Hurtado Albir. 2002. Translation techniques revisited: A dynamic and functionalist approach. *Meta*, 47(4):498–512.

Yongyu Mu, Abudurexiti Reheman, Zhiquan Cao, Yuchun Fan, Bei Li, Yinqiao Li, Tong Xiao, Chunliang Zhang, and Jingbo Zhu. 2023. Augmenting large language model translators via translation memories. In *Findings of the Association for Computational Linguistics: ACL 2023*, pages 10287–10299, Toronto, Canada. Association for Computational Linguistics.

Hongbin Na, Zimu Wang, Mieradilijiang Maimaiti, Tong Chen, Wei Wang, Tao Shen, and Ling Chen. 2024. Rethinking human-like translation strategy: Integrating drift-diffusion model with large language models for machine translation. *Preprint*, arXiv:2402.10699.

Kishore Papineni, Salim Roukos, Todd Ward, and Wei-Jing Zhu. 2002. Bleu: a method for automatic evaluation of machine translation. In *Proceedings of the 40th Annual Meeting of the Association for Computational Linguistics*, pages 311–318, Philadelphia, Pennsylvania, USA. Association for Computational Linguistics.

Maja Popović. 2017. chrF++: words helping character n-grams. In *Proceedings of the Second Conference on Machine Translation*, pages 612–618, Copenhagen, Denmark. Association for Computational Linguistics.

Matt Post. 2018. A call for clarity in reporting BLEU scores. In *Proceedings of the Third Conference on Machine Translation: Research Papers*, pages 186–191, Brussels, Belgium. Association for Computational Linguistics.

Vikas Raunak, Arul Menezes, Matt Post, and Hany Hassan. 2023a. Do GPTs produce less literal translations? In *Proceedings of the 61st Annual Meeting of the Association for Computational Linguistics (Volume 2: Short Papers)*, pages 1041–1050, Toronto, Canada. Association for Computational Linguistics.

Vikas Raunak, Amr Sharaf, Yiren Wang, Hany Awadalla, and Arul Menezes. 2023b. Leveraging GPT-4 for automatic translation post-editing. In *Findings of the Association for Computational Linguistics: EMNLP 2023*, pages 12009–12024, Singapore. Association for Computational Linguistics.

Ricardo Rei, Nuno M. Guerreiro, JosÃ© Pombal, Daan van Stigt, Marcos Treviso, Luisa Coheur, José G. C. de Souza, and André Martins. 2023. Scaling up CometKiwi: Unbabel-IST 2023 submission for the quality estimation shared task. In *Proceedings of the Eighth Conference on Machine Translation*, pages 841–848, Singapore. Association for Computational Linguistics.

Ricardo Rei, Craig Stewart, Ana C Farinha, and Alon Lavie. 2020. COMET: A neural framework for MT evaluation. In *Proceedings of the 2020 Conference on Empirical Methods in Natural Language Processing (EMNLP)*, pages 2685–2702, Online. Association for Computational Linguistics.

Ricardo Rei, Marcos Treviso, Nuno M. Guerreiro, Chrysoula Zerva, Ana C Farinha, Christine Maroti, José G. C. de Souza, Taisiya Glushkova, Duarte Alves, Luisa Coheur, Alon Lavie, and André F. T. Martins. 2022. CometKiwi: IST-unbabel 2022 submission for the quality estimation shared task. In *Proceedings of the Seventh Conference on Machine Translation (WMT)*, pages 634–645, Abu Dhabi, United Arab Emirates (Hybrid). Association for Computational Linguistics.

Thibault Sellam, Dipanjan Das, and Ankur Parikh. 2020. BLEURT: Learning robust metrics for text generation. In *Proceedings of the 58th Annual Meeting of the Association for Computational Linguistics*, pages 7881–7892, Online. Association for Computational Linguistics.

Sai Cheong Siu. 2023. Chatgpt and gpt-4 for professional translators: Exploring the potential of large language models in translation. *Available at SSRN 4448091*.

Kenan Tang. 2022. Petci: A parallel english translation dataset of chinese idioms. *arXiv preprint arXiv:2202.09509*.

Zhen Tao, Dinghao Xi, Zhiyu Li, Liumin Tang, and Wei Xu. 2024. Cat-llm: Prompting large language models with text style definition for chinese article-style transfer. *Preprint*, arXiv:2401.05707.

Katherine Thai, Marzena Karpinska, Kalpesh Krishna, Bill Ray, Moira Inghilleri, John Wieting, and Mohit Iyyer. 2022. Exploring document-level literary machine translation with parallel paragraphs from world literature. In *Proceedings of the 2022 Conference on Empirical Methods in Natural Language Processing*, pages 9882–9902, Abu Dhabi, United Arab Emirates. Association for Computational Linguistics.

Hugo Touvron, Thibaut Lavril, Gautier Izacard, Xavier Martinet, Marie-Anne Lachaux, Timoth'l'e Lacroix, Baptiste Rozi'Íre, Naman Goyal, Eric Hambro, Faisal Azhar, Aurelien Rodriguez, Armand Joulin, Edouard Grave, and Guillaume Lample. 2023. Llama: Open and efficient foundation language models. *Preprint*, arXiv:2302.13971.

Danqing Wang and Lei Li. 2023. Learning from mistakes via cooperative study assistant for large language models. In *Proceedings of the 2023 Conference on Empirical Methods in Natural Language Processing*, pages 10667–10685, Singapore. Association for Computational Linguistics.

Longyue Wang, Zhaopeng Tu, Yan Gu, Siyou Liu, Dian Yu, Qingsong Ma, Chenyang Lyu, Liting Zhou, Chao-Hong Liu, Yufeng Ma, Weiyu Chen, Yvette Graham, Bonnie Webber, Philipp Koehn, Andy Way, Yulin Yuan, and Shuming Shi. 2023. Findings of the WMT 2023 shared task on discourse-level literary translation: A fresh orb in the cosmos of LLMs. In *Proceedings of the Eighth Conference on Machine Translation*, pages 55–67, Singapore. Association for Computational Linguistics.

Binwei Yao, Ming Jiang, Diyi Yang, and Junjie Hu. 2023. Empowering llm-based machine translation with cultural awareness. *Preprint*, arXiv:2305.14328.

A Resources

In this section, we compare alternative resources with the ones we chose.

A.1 Dictionaries

The dictionaries we used contain 4,310 idioms for Chinese, 2440 for Japanese, and 2,316 for Korean. These dictionaries are all available for public use. While other larger idiom dictionaries are available[8], our primary focus in this work was not a comprehensive coverage of all idioms in a language. The dictionaries we used should have included the idioms that are most frequently used.

It is worth noting that East Asian idioms include more than just the 4-character category. One example is the *xiehouyu* in Chinese that has a different format. While we did not consider these other categories for experiments, our methods are applicable.

An interesting question is whether we can retrieve the idioms from GPT-4 just like we can retrieve the translations. To mine idioms, we asked GPT-4 to list a given number of idioms with a given initial. The initials are all valid *pinyin* syllables in Chinese, and they can be written as one or more roman letters (e.g. "a", "an", and "ang"). We obtained a list of 416 *pinyin* syllables from Wikipedia[9]. One syllable might be a prefix of another, so different idiom lists returned by GPT-4 might partially overlap with each other. Based on various idiom dictionaries used in previous work in the NLP community (Li et al., 2024), we estimated that the total number of frequently used Chinese idioms does not exceed 10K. Hence, for each initial, we asked GPT-4 to list 200 idioms. We expected the sufficiently large number of queries would give

[8]https://github.com/pwxcoo/chinese-xinhua/blob/master/data/idiom.json

[9]https://en.wikipedia.org/wiki/Comparison_of_Standard_Chinese_transcription_systems

us a comprehensive list after deduplication. Furthermore, for each initial, we made 5 queries with different random seeds to improve stability, as we observed that GPT-4 produced results in some runs that were much worse than in other runs.

We found that when listing idioms, GPT-4 tended to provide explanation or pronunciation of the idioms. Since these information are irrelevant for the listing task and significantly increase the output length, we asked GPT-4 to only list idioms without explaining them. We also found that when we did not explicitly require GPT-4 to list different idioms, GPT-4 tended to repeat a small set of idioms during listing. Hence, we explicitly asked GPT-4 to list different idioms.

Still, with the constraints in the prompt, GPT-4 occasionally produced undesirable content. We summarize the failure patterns below.

First, not every query returned with 200 results. This can be expected, as there do not exist 200 idioms for some initials. However, we saw a large number of queries stopping at exactly 100 results. This indicated that GPT-4 was not interpreting the number in the instruction with full precision.

Secondly, when given a certain initial, GPT-4 returned idioms with this initial in the beginning of the list, but idioms with different initials appeared later in the list. This was another example showing that the instruction was not precisely understood, even for the very simple task of listing.

Thirdly, a majority of the returned expressions were not Chinese idioms. These fake idioms could be divided into two categories. For a idiom in the first category, when we asked GPT-4 whether this is a Chinese idiom, GPT-4 successfully identified the idiom to be fake. Similar to the previous failure pattern, this indicates that the classification ability of GPT-4 is weaker during listing than when classifying a single example. Some examples of the first category included general multi-word expressions (e.g. "半导体照明") and real idioms with a single character replaced (e.g. "按甲不动" from "按兵不动"). The second category was more intriguing, as GPT-4 identified the fake idioms to be real (e.g. "落翅螳螂"). In this category, the seemingly plausible idioms are constructed in a very similar way as real idioms. Hence, we manually selected 50 such idioms when we tested the translation strategies.

A.2 Parallel Corpora

We have observed a low occurrence rate of idioms in large scale parallel corpora, for example the training set of WMT'23 (Kocmi et al., 2023). Idioms appear more often in literary text. However, due to copyright restrictions, the available literary parallel corpus is usually very small (Thai et al., 2022). The largest literary parallel corpus we have found is the BWB corpus (Jiang et al., 2022), which is a publicly available dataset of the English translation of Chinese web novels. Furthermore, due to sentence rearranging in literary translation, the smallest unit of a source-target pair in BWB is paragraphs. This makes it difficult to use BWB as a baseline to compare with the translations we get. Hence, we only used BWB to estimate the frequency ranking of idioms, where the frequency of an idiom is defined as the number of sentence pairs that contain this idiom. For the Chinese-English translation direction, GuoFeng (Wang et al., 2023) is another large-scale literary parallel corpus. Since the dataset is also derived from web novels, we do not assume a large difference when the dataset is used for frequency estimation instead of BWB.

A.3 Evaluation Metrics

Translation quality estimation has long been studied in the NLP community. Currently, the popular metrics are COMET (Rei et al., 2020), COMETKIWI (Rei et al., 2022), BLEURT (Sellam et al., 2020), BLEU (Papineni et al., 2002), and chrF++ (Popović, 2017)[10]. Among these metrics, the reference-free COMETKIWI is the most suitable for a creative generation task. We used the `wmt-23-cometkiwi-da-xxl` version of COMETKIWI (Rei et al., 2023).

LLM-based metrics have been shown to perform well on text summarization and dialog generation (Liu et al., 2023). For translation, LLMs were also applied to generate scores and textual evaluations (Kocmi and Federmann, 2023; Fernandes et al., 2023) based on MQM (Freitag et al., 2021). These work validated our choice of GPT-4 as an automatic evaluator of translation quality. We also explored the novel setting of evaluating creativity of translation, an aspect not covered by MQM.

Imperfect as they are, LLM-based automatic metrics are suitable for the assumed purpose of our dataset. We would like to provide a set of relatively good translations for a human translator to choose from. The automatic metrics reduce the cost of retrieving translations from LLMs and the time of human translators reading through the list.

[10]Both BLEU and chrF++ are implemented in SacreBLEU (Post, 2018).

Automatic metrics may produce false negatives (high-quality translations that are excluded due to low scores) and false positives (low-quality translations that are chosen due to high scores). However, on the one hand, false negatives are not concerning due to the sheer number of translations we are able to retrieve. On the other hand, false positives can be easily identified by human translators. Hence, we chose automatic metrics to help data collection.

A.4 Large Language Models

LLMs other than GPT-4 have been widely used on translation-related tasks. Some examples are Claude-2[11], Gemini-Pro[12], Flan-T5 (Chung et al., 2024), GPT-NeoX (Black et al., 2022), and LLaMA (Touvron et al., 2023). Since the prompting strategies we used in this work is model agnostic, it would be beneficial to use them on any model from the rapidly evolving set of LLMs. There is not a wide agreement on which model to choose. A consistent gap in translation quality between models was reported under some prompting strategies (Wang and Li, 2023) and datasets but not others (Feng et al., 2024b).

B Prompts

In this section, we list all prompts we used. While a variety of prompts have been used for translation (Table 5), we used the prompts that more directly describes both our idiom translation task and relevant translation instructions. For all the prompts, we use a temperature of 1.0. In our pilot study, we observe that changing the temperature in the API call does not produce meaningful variations in the generated translations. The total cost of all GPT-related experiments in this paper, including pilot studies, was $480.55.

B.1 Idioms

For Chinese idiom mining, we used the prompt:

- Give 200 Chinese idioms that begin with `<PINYIN>`. Only list idioms. Do not explain them. No duplicates.

Here, `<PINYIN>` is chosen from a list of 416 *pinyin* syllables obtained from Wikipedia[13].

[11]`https://www.anthropic.com/index/claude-2`

[12]`https://cloud.google.com/vertex-ai/docs/generativeai/learn/models`

[13]`https://en.wikipedia.org/wiki/Comparison_of_Standard_Chinese_transcription_systems`

For checking if a result is a true Chinese idiom, we used the prompt:

- Is `<IDIOM>` a Chinese idiom? Output yes or no.

For explanation generation, we used the prompt:

- Is `<PLAUSIBLE IDIOM>` a Chinese idiom? Please explain.

B.2 Sentences

For sentence generation, we used the prompt:

- Can you make 10 `<LANGUAGE>` sentences with the `<LANGUAGE>` idiom `<IDIOM>`? Only list sentences. Do not explain.

For plausible Chinese, we use "Chinese" as the `<LANGUAGE>`.

B.3 Zero-Shot Translations

For zero-shot translation, we used the prompts in Table 6.

B.4 Few-Shot Translations

For few-shot translation, we used the prompts in Table 7. The example sentence pairs are randomly chosen from a set of sentence pairs with highly creative translations.

B.5 Paragraph Translations

For instruction generation, we used the following 3 prompts:

- If you are asked to translate a paragraph that contains a `<LANGUAGE>` idiom, what would you do to ensure that the translation of the idiom is faithful?

- If you are asked to translate a paragraph that contains a `<LANGUAGE>` idiom, what would you do to ensure that the translation of the idiom is creative?

- If you are asked to translate a paragraph that contains a `<LANGUAGE>` idiom, what would you do to ensure that the translation of the idiom matches the theme of its context?

For paragraph translation, we used the prompts in Table 8.

Reference	Strategies
Jiao et al. (2023)	ChatGPT generated templates
Siu (2023)	Instructions in multi-turn dialogs
Lyu et al. (2024)	Specifying a poetic style
He et al. (2023)	Providing keywords, topics, or demonstrations mined by ChatGPT
Na et al. (2024)	Using Skopos, functional equivalence, or text typology theory
Tao et al. (2024)	Specifying style by several word-level and sentence-level statistics
Mu et al. (2023)	Extracting most similar sentences from a translation database
Yao et al. (2023)	Providing the whole sentence and a literal translation of a cultural-specific entity

Table 5: A summary of prompting strategies for translation.

Name	Prompt
BASELINE	Please translate the following sentence from <LANGUAGE> to English: <SENTENCE>
DIVERSITY EXPLICIT	Please generate 5 different translations of the following sentence from <LANGUAGE> to English: <SENTENCE>
DIVERSITY DIALOG	Please generate another 5 different translations.
ZERO-SHOT CREATIVELY	Please creatively translate the following sentence from <LANGUAGE> to English: <SENTENCE>
CONTEXT EXPLICIT	The sentence below comes from <GENRE>. Please translate it from <LANGUAGE> to English: <SENTENCE>
ANALOGY NATURAL	Please translate the following sentence from <LANGUAGE> to English: <SENTENCE> In the translation, please use an analogy commonly used in English.
ANALOGY CREATIVE	Please translate the following sentence from <LANGUAGE> to English: <SENTENCE> In the translation, please create a new analogy that has not been commonly used in English.
SHUFFLE ORDER	Please translate the following sentence from <LANGUAGE> to English: <SENTENCE> Please try to change the order of clauses to make the translation more natural.
SUCCINCT	Please translate the following sentence from <LANGUAGE> to English: <SENTENCE> Please translate the <LANGUAGE> idiom appeared in the sentence as succinctly as possible.
TWO-STEP	Please rewrite the following sentence in <LANGUAGE> without using a <LANGUAGE> idiom: <SENTENCE> Please translate the rewritten sentence to English.
DISCONTINUOUS 1	Please translate the following sentence from <LANGUAGE> to English: <SENTENCE> Please do not use a continuous span to translate the <LANGUAGE> idiom appeared in the sentence.
DISCONTINUOUS 2	Please translate the following sentence from <LANGUAGE> to English: <SENTENCE> Please do not use a multi-word expression to translate the <LANGUAGE> idiom appeared in the sentence.

Table 6: The prompts we used for zero-shot translation.

Name	Prompt
FEW-SHOT	Please translate the following sentences from <LANGUAGE> to English: <LANGUAGE>: <SOURCE 1> English: <TARGET 1> <LANGUAGE>: <SOURCE 2> English: <TARGET 2> <LANGUAGE>: <SOURCE 3> English: <TARGET 3> <LANGUAGE>: <SOURCE 4> English: <TARGET 4> <LANGUAGE>: <SOURCE 5> English: <TARGET 5> <LANGUAGE>: <SENTENCE> English:
FEW-SHOT CREATIVELY	Please creatively translate the following sentences from <LANGUAGE> to English: <LANGUAGE>: <SOURCE 1> English: <TARGET 1> <LANGUAGE>: <SOURCE 2> English: <TARGET 2> <LANGUAGE>: <SOURCE 3> English: <TARGET 3> <LANGUAGE>: <SOURCE 4> English: <TARGET 4> <LANGUAGE>: <SOURCE 5> English: <TARGET 5> <LANGUAGE>: <SENTENCE> English:

Table 7: The prompts we used for few-shot translation.

B.6 Span Extraction

For span extraction, we used the following prompt:

- Given the English translation of the <LANGUAGE> sentence, please only output the span that corresponds to the <LANGUAGE> idiom.
  <LANGUAGE> sentence: <SOURCE>
  English translation: <TARGET>
  <LANGUAGE> idiom: <IDIOM>
  Span:

We only tested the prompt on Chinese sentences.

B.7 Automatic Evaluation

For automatic evaluation of faithfulness, we used the following prompt:

- Please rate the faithfulness of the following idiom translation within a sentence.
  Idiom to be translated: <IDIOM>
  Original sentence containing this idiom: <SOURCE>
  Translation: <TARGET>
  Your faithfulness rating should be a score from 1 to 5, where 1 is not faithful at all and 5 is perfectly faithful. Return a single number as your rating.

For automatic evaluation of creativity, we used the following prompt:

- Please rate the creativity of the following idiom translation within a sentence.
  Idiom to be translated: <IDIOM>
  Original sentence containing this idiom: <SOURCE>
  Translation: <TARGET>
  Your creativity rating should be a score from 1 to 5, where 1 is not creative at all (just plain language) and 5 is perfectly creative. Return a single number as your rating.

C Cleaning and Parsing

In this section, we list the details for cleaning and parsing the model output.

C.1 Sentences

GPT-4 failed to generate sentences for very few idioms (4 out of all idioms). In these cases, GPT-4 was unable to identify the given idiom as a real word. Interestingly, this happened for real idioms, but not plausible idioms. For convenience of implementation, we save 10 empty sentences to the file when sentences are not generated.

Another failure pattern was that GPT-4 failed to include the idiom in the sentence. In these cases,

Name	Prompt
BASELINE	Please translate the following paragraph from <LANGUAGE> to English. <PARAGRAPH>
FAITHFUL SIMPLE	Please translate the following paragraph from <LANGUAGE> to English. Please translate the idiom <IDIOM> faithfully. Do not explain. <PARAGRAPH>
CREATIVE SIMPLE	Please translate the following paragraph from <LANGUAGE> to English. Please translate the idiom <IDIOM> creatively. Do not explain. <PARAGRAPH>
THEME SIMPLE	Please translate the following paragraph from <LANGUAGE> to English. Please translate the idiom <IDIOM> in a way that matches the theme. Do not explain. <PARAGRAPH>
FAITHFUL CoT	Please translate the following paragraph from <LANGUAGE> to English. Please translate the idiom <IDIOM> faithfully. Do not explain. <PARAGRAPH> Please follow the instructions below: <FAITHFUL INSTRUCTIONS>
CREATIVE CoT	Please translate the following paragraph from <LANGUAGE> to English. Please translate the idiom <IDIOM> creatively. Do not explain. <PARAGRAPH> Please follow the instructions below: <CREATIVE INSTRUCTIONS>
THEME CoT	Please translate the following paragraph from <LANGUAGE> to English. Please translate the idiom <IDIOM> in a way that matches the theme. Do not explain. <PARAGRAPH> Please follow the instructions below: <THEME INSTRUCTIONS>
FAITHFUL MULTI-TURN	Please translate the following paragraph from <LANGUAGE> to English. Please translate the idiom <IDIOM> faithfully. Do not explain. <PARAGRAPH>
CREATIVE MULTI-TURN	Could you provide an alternative translation of the paragraph, where the idiom is translated more creatively? The translation you provided has been widely used elsewhere.
THEME MULTI-TURN	Could you provide an alternative translation of the paragraph, where the idiom is translated with words that better match the context? The translation you provided can be used verbatim in a different context.

Table 8: The prompts we used for paragraph translation.

GPT-4 split the idiom into two parts, or used synonyms to represent the meaning of the idiom. The statistics for all languages are listed in Table 9.

C.2 Translations (Sentences)

In general, the output translations are clean. In the cases where GPT-4 was prompted to generate multiple translations in a single response, we parsed the response to get the list of translations. For the succinct prompt, GPT-4 tended to provide an explanation, which we removed from the response to get the clean translation.

C.3 Scores

GPT-3.5 generated scores in different formats, including different prefixes and suffixes. We observed that all the irrelevant output can be cleaned by taking the first digit appearing in the response string as the score.

C.4 Auto-CoT Instructions

We repeatedly asked GPT-4 for translation instructions. Given the same prompt, GPT-4 returned different steps. The number of steps ranged from 6 to 8. The name and the description of each step also differed. However, each different set of steps from a single response was reasonable. Hence, for each combination of aspect and language, we only used one response as the Auto-CoT instruction.

C.5 Paragraphs

GPT-4 sometimes does not include the sentence verbatim in the paragraph. This is due to punctuation and language-specific phenomena, such as conjugation in Japanese and Korean. However, in most cases, the paragraph contains the idiom. The statistics for all languages are listed in Table 10.

C.6 Translations (Paragraphs)

No noise was observed.

C.7 Spans

GPT-4 was able to locate precisely the span in the translated sentence that corresponds to the idiom in the original sentence. The identified span is a substring of the translated sentence for 1994 out of 2000 Chinese-English sentence pairs, translated using the optimal strategies. The few failures were due to the change in capitalization and punctuation.

D More Results

In this section, we show more examples from our results. No spans are highlighted for these examples, as we did not perform manual labeling and did not run the span queries (Appendix B.6) for these translations. The total number of sentence translations is 13,500 for each language. For Chinese, we further generate 20,000 translations with Pareto-optimal strategies. For each translation, we generate 5 faithfulness and 5 creativity scores.

D.1 Sentence Translations

We show more translations for all languages we used in Tables 11 (Chinese), 12 (Japanese), 13 (Korean), and 14 (plausible Chinese). All other translations can be found in the published data. The total number of paragraph translations is 800 for each language.

D.2 Paragraph Translations

For the paragraph pipeline, we show more examples in Tables 15 (Chinese), 16 (Japanese), 17, and 18 (plausible Chinese). The paragraphs were generated with the same sentences in Appendix D.1. All shown examples are in the genre "a news report" (Section 2), while examples in the other genre can be found in the published data.

E Scores

We summarize the faithfulness and creativity scores for all languages and all strategies in Table 19. We also visualize the scores using a heat map in Figure 3 and scatter plots in Figure 4.

Language	# Idioms	# Sentences	# w/ Idiom	% w/ Idiom
Chinese	4310	43100	42873	99.71
Japanese	2440	24400	24247	99.37
Korean	2316	23160	22943	99.06
Plausible Chinese	50	500	495	99.00

Table 9: The statistics for noise in sentence generation.

Language	# Paragraphs	# w/ Idiom	% w/ Idiom	# w/ Sentence	% w/ Sentence
Chinese	80	80	100.00	51	63.75
Japanese	80	79	98.75	37	46.25
Korean	80	78	97.50	36	45.00
Plausible Chinese	80	73	91.25	56	70.00

Table 10: The statistics for noise in paragraph generation.

Method	Sentence	Faithfulness	Creativity
ORIGINAL	他们通过威逼利诱，想要我放弃诉讼。	N/A	N/A
GOOGLE	They used threats and inducements to try to get me to drop the lawsuit.	4.8	3.8
DEEPL	They wanted me to drop the lawsuit through bullying.	2.2	2.6
BASELINE	They tried to get me to drop the lawsuit through threats and inducements.	4.2	3.8
DIVERSITY EXPLICIT	Through intimidation and temptation, they want me to give up the lawsuit.	5.0	3.6
DIVERSITY EXPLICIT	They employed threats and bribes, trying to get me to abandon the lawsuit.	4.4	4.0
DIVERSITY EXPLICIT	By wielding both threats and incentives, they aim to make me drop the lawsuit.	4.4	4.0
DIVERSITY EXPLICIT	They attempted to make me forsake the lawsuit by means of coercion and enticement.	4.4	3.2
DIVERSITY EXPLICIT	They're using a mix of scare tactics and promises in hopes I'll relinquish the lawsuit.	4.0	4.2
DIVERSITY DIALOG	They are using a combination of threats and rewards to persuade me to withdraw from the lawsuit.	4.6	4.0
DIVERSITY DIALOG	With a strategy of intimidation and allure, they seek to have me forego the lawsuit.	4.0	4.0
DIVERSITY DIALOG	They're applying pressure and offering inducements, hoping I will abandon my legal action.	4.8	4.0
DIVERSITY DIALOG	By employing coercion and temptation, their goal is for me to give up my lawsuit.	4.2	3.0
DIVERSITY DIALOG	Through both menacing and luring tactics, they wish for me to relinquish the lawsuit.	4.4	4.0
ZERO-SHOT CREATIVELY	Through a mix of threats and temptations, they sought to make me abandon my lawsuit.	4.6	4.0
CONTEXT EXPLICIT	They tried to make me give up the lawsuit through threats and bribes.	4.4	2.8
CONTEXT EXPLICIT	They, through intimidation and inducement, want me to give up the lawsuit.	4.6	3.0
CONTEXT EXPLICIT	They tried to make me give up the lawsuit through threats and bribes.	4.6	3.0
CONTEXT EXPLICIT	They tried to make me give up the lawsuit through intimidation and bribery.	4.6	3.2
ANALOGY NATURAL	They tried to make me drop the lawsuit through a carrot and stick approach.	4.0	4.0
ANALOGY CREATIVE	They tried to make me drop the lawsuit by dangling carrots laced with threats, like offering honey wrapped in thorns.	3.6	4.2
SHUFFLE ORDER	They tried to get me to drop the lawsuit by using threats and bribes.	4.0	3.8
SUCCINCT	They, through threats and bribes, want me to give up the lawsuit.	4.2	3.0
TWO-STEP	They used threats and temptations, trying to make me give up the lawsuit.	4.0	3.6
DISCONTINUOUS 1	They, through threats and promises, want me to give up the lawsuit.	4.8	3.0
DISCONTINUOUS 2	They want me to give up the lawsuit by coercing and bribing.	4.0	2.8
FEW-SHOT	They tried to make me give up the lawsuit through threats and bribes.	4.6	3.2
FEW-SHOT CREATIVELY	They attempted to sway my resolve through a mix of threats and temptations, hoping I would abandon the lawsuit.	5.0	4.0

Table 11: The example translations for Chinese.

Method	Sentence	Faithfulness	Creativity
ORIGINAL	私たちの小さなプロジェクトが、まさに燎原之火となり、急速に広がりました	N/A	N/A
GOOGLE	Our small project became a wildfire and spread rapidly.	4.2	4.0
DEEPL	Our little project became a veritable bonfire and spread rapidly.	2.8	4.0
BASELINE	Our small project, just like a spark in a field, rapidly spread far and wide.	3.4	4.2
DIVERSITY EXPLICIT	Our small project has indeed become a spark that quickly spread like wildfire.	4.4	4.2
DIVERSITY EXPLICIT	Our modest project has truly become a blaze that rapidly expanded.	3.6	3.8
DIVERSITY EXPLICIT	The little project of ours has indeed turned into a raging fire, spreading swiftly.	4.0	4.0
DIVERSITY EXPLICIT	Our small project has indeed become a prairie fire, spreading rapidly.	4.8	4.2
DIVERSITY EXPLICIT	Our minor project quickly became a spark that turned into a widespread inferno.	2.8	4.0
DIVERSITY DIALOG	Our little project has truly blossomed into a widespread blaze, spreading quickly.	2.8	3.8
DIVERSITY DIALOG	Our small initiative indeed became a conflagration that rapidly expanded.	4.4	4.0
DIVERSITY DIALOG	The small project we started has really caught on like wildfire, spreading rapidly.	4.4	4.0
DIVERSITY DIALOG	Our humble project turned into a blazing fire, quickly covering ground.	4.4	4.0
DIVERSITY DIALOG	Our tiny project has, indeed, turned into a spark that has rapidly spread far and wide.	3.6	4.0
ZERO-SHOT CREATIVELY	Our humble project, akin to a spark in a dry field, swiftly ignited, spreading far and wide with rapid fervor.	4.4	4.2
CONTEXT EXPLICIT	Our small project has indeed become a spark that quickly spread like wildfire.	4.2	4.2
CONTEXT EXPLICIT	Our small project became like a spark in a prairie, spreading rapidly.	3.2	4.0
CONTEXT EXPLICIT	Our small project has indeed become a spark that ignites the plains, spreading rapidly.	3.2	4.2
CONTEXT EXPLICIT	Our small project became like a spark in a prairie, spreading rapidly.	3.4	4.0
ANALOGY NATURAL	Our little project caught fire like wildfire and spread rapidly.	3.6	4.2
ANALOGY CREATIVE	Our modest project, just like a spark in a sea of whispers, quickly spread far and wide.	1.6	4.2
SHUFFLE ORDER	Our small project has indeed become a blaze that quickly spread far and wide.	4.0	3.6
SUCCINCT	Our small project has indeed become a spark that started a prairie fire, spreading rapidly.	5.0	4.4
TWO-STEP	Our small project really spread rapidly.	1.8	2.0
DISCONTINUOUS 1	Our small project, just like a spark in a field, rapidly spread far and wide.	3.4	4.2
DISCONTINUOUS 2	Our small project has indeed become a wildfire and spread rapidly.	4.2	3.8
FEW-SHOT	Our small project became like a wildfire, spreading rapidly.	4.6	4.0
FEW-SHOT CREATIVELY	Our modest project became a wildfire, spreading rapidly far and wide.	4.0	4.0

Table 12: The example translations for Japanese.

Method	Sentence	Faithfulness	Creativity
ORIGINAL	진짜 그 사람이 싫어서 안 만나는 건지, 아니면 담인인지 모르겠어.	N/A	N/A
GOOGLE	I don't know if I'm not dating that person because I really hate him, or if he's just a temperamental person.	2.2	3.6
DEEPL	I don't know if I'm not seeing him because I really don't like him, or if he's a dummy.	2.0	3.8
BASELINE	I'm not sure if it's really because I dislike that person that I don't meet them, or if it's because I'm just busy.	3.2	3.0
DIVERSITY EXPLICIT	I'm not sure if it's because I really dislike that person or if I'm just being indifferent.	3.6	3.8
DIVERSITY EXPLICIT	I can't tell if I'm not meeting them because I really hate them, or if I'm just unbothered.	3.6	4.0
DIVERSITY EXPLICIT	It's unclear whether I'm avoiding them because I genuinely don't like them, or if I'm just being nonchalant.	3.0	4.0
DIVERSITY EXPLICIT	I'm uncertain if my not seeing them is due to real distaste or simply indifference.	4.0	4.0
DIVERSITY EXPLICIT	It's hard to say whether my avoidance is because of genuine dislike or if I am just indifferent.	4.0	4.0
DIVERSITY DIALOG	I can't figure out if my refusal to meet is because I truly detest that person, or if it's just apathy.	4.2	3.6
DIVERSITY DIALOG	I'm unsure whether my avoidance is rooted in real animosity towards that person or mere indifference.	4.4	4.0
DIVERSITY DIALOG	It's difficult to determine if I'm not seeing them because I genuinely loathe them, or if I'm just detached.	3.6	4.0
DIVERSITY DIALOG	I'm puzzled whether my lack of desire to meet stems from actual aversion or simply from being disinterested.	3.8	4.2
DIVERSITY DIALOG	I find it challenging to discern if my avoidance is due to a genuine dislike or if it's just a matter of being indifferent.	4.2	4.0
ZERO-SHOT CREATIVELY	I can't tell if they're genuinely avoiding that person because they dislike them, or if it's because they're shy.	3.8	4.0
CONTEXT EXPLICIT	I'm not sure if it's because they really dislike that person that they're not meeting, or if it's because they're just playing hard to get.	4.0	4.2
CONTEXT EXPLICIT	I can't tell if it's because they really dislike that person that they're not meeting, or if it's because they're playing hard to get.	3.8	3.8
CONTEXT EXPLICIT	I can't tell if they're really avoiding meeting because they dislike that person, or if they're just busy.	3.6	3.4
CONTEXT EXPLICIT	I'm not sure if it's because they really dislike that person or if it's because they are just busy.	3.6	3.6
ANALOGY NATURAL	"I can't tell if they're really avoiding someone because they dislike them, or if they're just playing hard to get."	3.4	4.0
ANALOGY CREATIVE	"I can't tell if they're really avoiding meeting because they dislike that person, or if it's like trying to decipher the flavor of a mystery soda."	2.2	4.4
SHUFFLE ORDER	I can't tell if they're really avoiding meeting because they dislike that person, or if they're just busy.	3.8	3.4
SUCCINCT	I can't tell if it's really because they dislike that person that they're not meeting up, or if they're just playing hard to get.	4.0	4.0
TWO-STEP	I don't know if it's really because I dislike that person that I'm not meeting them, or if there is another reason.	4.2	3.2
DISCONTINUOUS 1	I can't tell if they're really not meeting because they dislike that person, or if it's because they're playing hard to get.	3.8	4.0
DISCONTINUOUS 2	I'm not sure if it's really because I don't like that person that I'm not meeting them, or if it's something else.	4.2	3.6
FEW-SHOT	I can't tell if they're not meeting because they genuinely dislike the person or if it's just an excuse.	4.0	4.0
FEW-SHOT CREATIVELY	I can't tell if it's genuinely because they dislike that person that they don't meet up, or if it's just an excuse.	4.0	3.8

Table 13: The example translations for Korean.

Method	Sentence	Faithfulness	Creativity
ORIGINAL	每年的春天，园子里春荷盛开，秋天则是秋菊竞艳。	N/A	N/A
GOOGLE	Every spring, lotus flowers bloom in the garden, and in autumn, chrysanthemums bloom.	3.2	2.2
DEEPL	Every spring, the garden is in full bloom with spring lotus, and in the fall, fall chrysanthemums compete.	4.2	4.0
BASELINE	Every spring, the garden is filled with blooming spring lotuses, while in autumn, it's the chrysanthemums that vie for beauty.	4.0	4.0
DIVERSITY EXPLICIT	Every spring, the garden blooms with spring lotuses, while in autumn, the chrysanthemums vie for beauty.	4.2	3.6
DIVERSITY EXPLICIT	In the garden, spring sees the lush blossoming of lotuses, and autumn showcases the competitive bloom of chrysanthemums.	4.0	4.0
DIVERSITY EXPLICIT	Yearly, spring brings the luxuriant opening of lotuses in the garden, and autumn displays the dazzling chrysanthemums.	3.2	3.8
DIVERSITY EXPLICIT	Every year, the springtime garden is filled with blooming lotuses, and autumn with the splendid display of chrysanthemums.	3.6	3.8
DIVERSITY EXPLICIT	The garden annually celebrates spring with the flourishing of lotuses, and autumn with the striking rivalry of chrysanthemums.	3.8	4.0
DIVERSITY DIALOG	Each spring, the garden is adorned with burgeoning lotuses, while autumn brings forth the competing beauty of chrysanthemums.	4.4	4.0
DIVERSITY DIALOG	Annually, the spring season witnesses the garden's lotuses in full bloom, followed by the chrysanthemums' vibrant display in autumn.	4.0	4.2
DIVERSITY DIALOG	The garden experiences a bounty of spring lotuses every year, and in autumn, the chrysanthemums burst into competitive radiance.	3.6	3.8
DIVERSITY DIALOG	Every spring, lotuses thrive in the garden, with autumn presenting a spectacle of chrysanthemums competing in splendor.	3.8	4.0
DIVERSITY DIALOG	In the garden, each year, spring is marked by the blossoming of lotuses and autumn by the riotous beauty of chrysanthemums in competition.	4.4	4.0
ZERO-SHOT CREATIVELY	Every spring, the garden blooms with vibrant spring lotus, while in autumn, the chrysanthemums vie in beauty.	3.8	4.0
CONTEXT EXPLICIT	Every spring, the lotus blooms abundantly in the garden, while in autumn, the chrysanthemums vie in beauty.	4.0	4.0
CONTEXT EXPLICIT	Every spring, the lotus blooms abundantly in the garden, while in autumn, the chrysanthemums compete in beauty.	4.0	4.0
CONTEXT EXPLICIT	Every spring, the lotus blooms abundantly in the garden, while in autumn, the chrysanthemums compete in beauty.	4.0	4.0
CONTEXT EXPLICIT	Every spring, the lotus blooms profusely in the garden, while in autumn, the chrysanthemums vie in beauty.	3.6	3.8
ANALOGY NATURAL	Every spring, the garden blooms with spring lotuses, much like a sea of blossoms, and in autumn, autumn chrysanthemums vie in beauty, akin to a painter's vibrant palette.	3.8	4.2
ANALOGY CREATIVE	In the springtime each year, the garden blossoms into a sea of spring lotuses, while in autumn, it transforms into a stage where autumn chrysanthemums vie for the spotlight.	3.6	4.2
SHUFFLE ORDER	Every spring, the lotus blossoms flourish in the garden, while in autumn, the chrysanthemums vie in beauty.	4.0	4.0
SUCCINCT	Every spring, the lotus flowers bloom in abundance in the garden, and in autumn, the chrysanthemums vie in beauty.	3.6	3.8
TWO-STEP	Every spring, the lotuses in the garden bloom in abundance; come autumn, it is the chrysanthemums' turn to bloom competitively.	3.6	4.0
DISCONTINUOUS 1	Every spring, the garden is in full bloom with spring lotuses, and in autumn, autumn chrysanthemums vie in beauty.	3.6	3.8
DISCONTINUOUS 2	Every spring, the garden is full of blooming lotuses, and in autumn, autumn chrysanthemums vie in beauty.	3.6	4.0
FEW-SHOT	Every spring, the garden blossoms with spring lotuses, while in autumn, the autumn chrysanthemums vie in beauty.	4.0	4.0
FEW-SHOT CREATIVELY	Every spring, the garden is a spectacle of blooming spring lotuses, while autumn boasts a competitive display of vibrant chrysanthemums.	4.0	4.2

Table 14: The example translations for plausible Chinese.

Method	Paragraph
ORIGINAL	在今日下午的新闻发布会上，被告李先生向媒体披露了一起备受关注的诉讼案件的最新进展。据李先生称，“他们通过威逼利诱，想要我放弃诉讼。”他详细说明了对方如何施加压力，试图迫使其撤销对公司不正当行为的指控。这起事件引起了公众的广泛关注，许多人表示，像李先生这样勇敢站出来揭露真相的行为，值得社会给予更多的支持和保护。
BASELINE	At this afternoon's press conference, Mr. Li, the defendant, disclosed the latest developments in a highly publicized lawsuit case to the media. According to Mr. Li, "They tried to make me give up the lawsuit through threats and bribes." He detailed how the other party applied pressure to force him to withdraw his accusations of the company's misconduct. This incident has garnered widespread public attention, with many people expressing that acts of bravery like Mr. Li's in exposing the truth deserve more societal support and protection.
FAITHFUL SIMPLE	At the press conference this afternoon, Mr. Li, the defendant, disclosed to the media the latest developments in a highly publicized lawsuit. According to Mr. Li, "They tried to make me give up the lawsuit through coercion and bribery." He detailed how the other party applied pressure, attempting to force him to withdraw his allegations of impropriety against the company. This incident has attracted widespread public attention, with many people stating that brave actions like Mr. Li's, in stepping forward to reveal the truth, deserve more societal support and protection.
CREATIVE SIMPLE	At this afternoon's press conference, Mr. Li, the defendant, disclosed to the media the latest developments in a highly publicized lawsuit. According to Mr. Li, "They tried to sway me with a mix of threats and temptations, wanting me to drop the lawsuit." He elaborated on how the other party applied pressure, attempting to force him to withdraw his accusations of improper conduct by the company. This incident has sparked widespread public interest, with many expressing that courageous acts like Mr. Li's in revealing the truth deserve more societal support and protection.
THEME SIMPLE	At this afternoon's press conference, Mr. Li, the defendant, revealed to the media the latest developments in a lawsuit that has garnered significant attention. According to Mr. Li, "They tried to strong-arm and entice me into dropping the lawsuit." He detailed how the other party applied pressure in an attempt to force him to withdraw his accusations of improper conduct by the company. This incident has sparked widespread public interest, with many expressing that courageous acts like Mr. Li's in exposing the truth deserve more societal support and protection.
FAITHFUL COT	At this afternoon's press conference, Mr. Li, the defendant, disclosed to the media the latest developments in a highly watched lawsuit. According to Mr. Li, "They tried to make me give up the lawsuit through threats and bribes." He detailed how the other party attempted to pressure him into withdrawing his allegations of the company's improper conduct. This incident has garnered widespread public attention, and many people believe that acts of bravery like Mr. Li's, in coming forward to reveal the truth, deserve more societal support and protection.
CREATIVE COT	At this afternoon's press conference, Mr. Li, the defendant, unveiled the latest developments in a highly anticipated lawsuit to the media. Mr. Li claimed, "They resorted to a mix of intimidation and enticement, aiming for me to drop the lawsuit." He elaborated on how the other party applied pressure, attempting to coerce him into retracting his allegations of misconduct against the company. This incident has drawn widespread public attention, with many voicing that courageous actions like Mr. Li's, stepping forward to expose the truth, deserve greater societal support and protection.
THEME COT	At the press conference this afternoon, Mr. Li, the defendant, disclosed to the media the latest developments in a highly publicized lawsuit. According to Mr. Li, ‘Ă‘IJThey tried to make me drop the lawsuit through a combination of threats and inducements.‘Ă‘İHe detailed how the other party applied pressure, attempting to force him to withdraw his allegations of misconduct against the company. This incident has attracted widespread public attention, with many people expressing that courageous actions like Mr. Li's, in revealing the truth, deserve more support and protection from society.
FAITHFUL MULTI-TURN	At this afternoon's press conference, Mr. Li, the defendant, disclosed to the media the latest developments in a highly publicized lawsuit. According to Mr. Li, "They tried to make me give up the lawsuit through coercion and bribery." He detailed how the other party applied pressure, attempting to force him to withdraw his allegations of impropriety against the company. This incident has attracted widespread public attention, with many people stating that brave actions like Mr. Li's, in stepping forward to reveal the truth, deserve more support and protection from society.
CREATIVE MULTI-TURN	At the news conference this afternoon, Mr. Li, the accused, unveiled to the press the latest developments in a closely watched lawsuit. Mr. Li claimed, "They attempted to sway me into dropping the lawsuit by a combination of threats and temptations." He elaborated on how the opposition exerted pressure, trying to compel him to rescind his accusations of misconduct against the company. The saga has captivated public interest, with many voicing that courageous disclosures like Mr. Li's merit greater societal endorsement and safeguarding.
THEME MULTI-TURN	In this afternoon's press conference, Mr. Li, the defendant, shared with the media the recent developments of a lawsuit that has captured widespread attention. Mr. Li stated, "They resorted to threats and allurements in an effort to make me abandon the lawsuit." He went into detail about how the other side applied pressure, aiming to make him withdraw his claims against the company's wrongful actions. The incident has sparked considerable public interest, with many expressing that the courageous act of coming forward like Mr. Li has done should be met with greater societal support and protection.

Table 15: The example paragraph translations for Chinese.

Method	Paragraph
ORIGINAL	日本、東京 - 地元の起業家たちが始めた画期的な取り組みが話題になっています。彼らの開発した環境に優しい再生可能エネルギー製品が予想外の成功を収め、大きな注目を集めています。「私たちの小さなプロジェクトが、まさに燎原之火となり、急速に広がりました。」と、プロジェクトリーダーは興奮を隠せません。この成功は、持続可能な開発と環境保護に関心が集まっている今、他の起業家や企業にも大きな刺激を与えています。
BASELINE	Japan, Tokyo - A groundbreaking initiative started by local entrepreneurs is gaining attention. Their development of environmentally friendly renewable energy products has achieved unexpected success and is drawing significant attention. "Our small project has truly become a blazing wildfire, spreading rapidly," says the project leader, unable to hide their excitement. This success is providing a major stimulus to other entrepreneurs and companies at a time when there is a growing focus on sustainable development and environmental protection.
FAITHFUL SIMPLE	Japan, Tokyo - An innovative initiative started by local entrepreneurs is making waves. Their development of eco-friendly renewable energy products has achieved unexpected success and garnered significant attention. "Our small project has indeed become a wildfire, spreading rapidly," the project leader could hardly contain his excitement. This success is providing a major stimulus to other entrepreneurs and companies at a time when interest in sustainable development and environmental protection is growing.
CREATIVE SIMPLE	Tokyo, Japan - A groundbreaking initiative started by local entrepreneurs is becoming a hot topic. Their development of environmentally friendly renewable energy products has achieved unexpected success and has drawn significant attention. "Our small project has, quite literally, become a wildfire, spreading rapidly," says the project leader, unable to hide his excitement. This success is providing great motivation to other entrepreneurs and corporations at a time when interest in sustainable development and environmental protection is growing.
THEME SIMPLE	Japan, Tokyo - An innovative initiative started by local entrepreneurs is becoming a hot topic. Their development of eco-friendly renewable energy products has achieved unexpected success and attracted significant attention. "Our small project has, indeed, spread like wildfire, rapidly expanding," the project leader said, unable to hide his excitement. This success is providing a substantial stimulus to other entrepreneurs and companies at a time when there is a growing focus on sustainable development and environmental protection.
FAITHFUL COT	Japan, Tokyo - A groundbreaking initiative started by local entrepreneurs is becoming a topic of conversation. Their developed environmentally friendly renewable energy products have achieved unexpected success and are attracting significant attention. "Our small project has indeed become a raging wildfire, spreading rapidly," says the project leader, unable to hide his excitement. This success is providing a substantial stimulus to other entrepreneurs and companies at a time when there is a strong focus on sustainable development and environmental protection.
CREATIVE COT	Tokyo, Japan - A groundbreaking initiative started by local entrepreneurs is making waves. Their development of environmentally friendly renewable energy products has achieved unexpected success and garnered significant attention. "Our small project has truly become a wildfire, spreading rapidly," says the project leader, unable to hide their excitement. This success has given a substantial boost to other entrepreneurs and companies at a time when there's a growing focus on sustainable development and environmental protection.
THEME COT	Japan, Tokyo - A groundbreaking initiative started by local entrepreneurs is making headlines. Their development of environmentally friendly renewable energy products has achieved unexpected success and garnered significant attention. "Our small project has indeed become a wildfire, spreading rapidly," the project leader could not hide their excitement. This success provides a major stimulus to other entrepreneurs and companies at a time when there is growing interest in sustainable development and environmental protection.
FAITHFUL MULTI-TURN	Japan, Tokyo - An innovative initiative started by local entrepreneurs is gaining attention. Their development of eco-friendly renewable energy products has achieved unexpected success and garnered significant interest. "Our small project has indeed become a wildfire, spreading rapidly," the project leader could hardly contain his excitement. This success is providing a major stimulus to other entrepreneurs and companies at a time when interest in sustainable development and environmental protection is growing.
CREATIVE MULTI-TURN	Japan, Tokyo - An innovative initiative started by local entrepreneurs is making waves. Their development of eco-friendly renewable energy products has unexpectedly soared to success, capturing widespread attention. "Our modest project has, quite literally, turned into a blaze across the prairie, expanding swiftly," the project leader is elated. This triumph is giving a significant boost to other entrepreneurs and corporations at a moment when the spotlight is on sustainable development and conservation of the environment.
THEME MULTI-TURN	Japan, Tokyo - A groundbreaking initiative launched by local entrepreneurs is creating a buzz. Their invention of eco-friendly renewable energy products has manifested into an unexpected triumph, attracting major interest. "Our humble project has indeed sparked a conflagration, spreading at an incredible pace," the project leader is visibly thrilled. This success is fueling a significant impetus among other entrepreneurs and businesses at a time when the focus on sustainable development and environmental preservation is intensifying.

Table 16: The example paragraph translations for Japanese.

Method	Paragraph
ORIGINAL	서울, 대한민국 - 지역 사회에서는 최근 한 개인의 대인 관계 문제가 관심사로 떠올랐습니다. 주변 사람들은 "진짜 그 사람이 싫어서 안 만나는 건지, 아니면 다른 진짜 이유가 있는 것인지 모르겠어" 라고 말하며, 이 문제에 대한 의견을 나누고 있습니다. 이 문제는 한 사람의 갑작스런 사회적 활동 감소와 그 이유에 대한 추측으로 인해 생겨났습니다. 해당 개인이나 그의 친구들은 현재 이와 관련된 공식적인 입장을 밝히지 않고 있으며, 이로 인해 더욱 많은 추측이 이어지고 있습니다. 지역사회는 이 문제에 대해 더 많은 정보를 원하며, 이에 대한 진실을 알기 위해 관심을 기울이고 있습니다.
BASELINE	Seoul, South Korea - A personal relationship issue of an individual has recently become a matter of interest in the community. People around are sharing their opinions, saying, "I'm not sure if they're really not meeting because they dislike that person, or if there's another real reason." This issue arose from speculation about the sudden decrease in one person's social activities and the reasons behind it. Neither the individual in question nor their friends have made an official statement regarding the matter, leading to even more speculation. The community is seeking more information on this issue and is keen to find out the truth.
FAITHFUL SIMPLE	Seoul, South Korea - In the local community, the personal relationship issue of an individual has recently become a matter of interest. People around are saying, "I don't know if it's really because they dislike that person and don't want to meet, or if there's another real reason," and are sharing their opinions on this issue. This issue arose due to a sudden decrease in one person's social activities and speculation about the reason. The individual in question or their friends have not made any official statements regarding this matter, leading to further speculation. The community wants more information about this issue and is keen to find out the truth.
CREATIVE SIMPLE	Seoul, South Korea - In the local community, the personal relationships of an individual have recently become a matter of interest. People around are saying, "I wonder if it's really because they dislike that person or if there's another real reason," as they share their opinions on this matter. The issue emerged due to a sudden decrease in social activities by the individual and speculation about the reasons behind it. Neither the individual in question nor their friends have made any official statement regarding this, leading to further speculation. The community is eager for more information on the matter and is paying close attention in hopes of uncovering the truth.
THEME SIMPLE	Seoul, South Korea - A personal relationship issue of an individual has recently become a topic of interest in the community. People around are saying, "I can't tell if they genuinely dislike the person and that's why they're not meeting, or if there's another real reason," and are sharing their opinions on this matter. This issue arose from sudden decreases in one person's social activities and speculation about the reasons behind it. Neither the individual in question nor their friends have made any official statement on the matter, leading to further speculation. The community wants more information on this issue and is keen to uncover the truth.
FAITHFUL COT	Seoul, South Korea - In the local community, the interpersonal relationship issue of an individual has recently arisen as a topic of interest. People around them are saying, 'Ă'IJI don't know if they are not meeting them because they really dislike the person, or if there's another real reason,'Ă'İsharing their opinions on this matter. This issue sprung up due to the sudden decrease in social activities of one person and the speculation about the reasons behind it. The individual in question or their friends have not officially addressed the matter, leading to even more speculation. The community wants more information on this issue and is paying attention to uncover the truth.
CREATIVE COT	Seoul, South Korea - In the local community, the interpersonal issues of an individual have recently become a hot topic. People around are saying, "I can't tell if they're actually giving the cold shoulder, or if there's some other real reason behind it," sharing their thoughts on the matter. This issue emerged due to a sudden decrease in social activities by an individual and the speculation around the reasons for such withdrawal. Neither the person in question nor their friends have made any official statements regarding the situation, leading to even more speculation. The community is eager for more information and is paying close attention in hopes of uncovering the truth.
THEME COT	Seoul, South Korea - A personal relationship issue of an individual has recently emerged as a concern within the community. People around are saying, "I don't know whether they're not meeting because they genuinely dislike each other, or if there's some other real reason," sharing their opinions on the matter. This issue arose from speculation about the sudden decrease in social activities of a person and the reasons behind it. Neither the individual in question nor their friends have made any official statement regarding this, leading to even more speculation. The community seeks more information on this issue, paying close attention to uncover the truth.
FAITHFUL MULTI-TURN	Seoul, South Korea - In the local community, the personal relationship issue of an individual has recently become a matter of interest. People around are saying, "I don't know if it's really because they dislike the person and don't want to meet, or if there's another real reason," and are sharing their opinions on this issue. This issue arose due to a sudden decrease in one person's social activities and speculation about the reason. The individual in question or their friends have not made any official statements regarding this matter, leading to further speculation. The community wants more information about this issue and is keen to find out the truth.
CREATIVE MULTI-TURN	Seoul, South Korea - A personal relationship dilemma involving an individual has recently captured the community's attention. Neighbors are speculating, "Is it genuinely because they despise the person so much they avoid meeting, or is there another underlying truth?" This conversation is buzzing around as people exchange views on the matter. Sparked by one individual's abrupt retreat from social engagements and the swirling guesses about its cause, this topic has become hot. Neither the person at the heart of the rumors nor their close associates have clarified their stance, fueling the rumor mill even more. The community is eager for more clarity on this issue, showing heightened interest to unearth the actual story.
THEME MULTI-TURN	Seoul, South Korea - In the local community, there's been a rising curiosity about an individual's inter-personal conflict. People around are left wondering, "Is it true aversion driving them apart or is there something deeper at play?" This speculation has grown from observing a notable drop in one's social interactions, sparking conversations. Neither the individual at the center of these rumors nor their confidants have come forward with any explanations, leading to evolving conjecture. The community is showing a keen interest, hoping to peel back the layers of this mystery and uncover the truth.

Table 17: The example paragraph translations for Korean.

Method	Paragraph
ORIGINAL	【环球新闻网】随着季节的更迭，大自然总是有着它独特的方式来展现生命之美。在我国南方的一个古老园林中，这种自然的循环得到了完美的体现。每年的春天，园子里春荷盛开，犹如一片片翠绿的玉盘，静静浮在水面上，吸引了无数游人驻足欣赏。而到了秋天，则是秋菊竞艳，黄、紫、白交织的菊花在秋风中摇曳生姿，成为这古园一道别样的风景线。这一切似乎在提醒着人们，无论世事如何变迁，自然的美好总是值得我们去珍惜和维护。
BASELINE	[Global News Network] As seasons change, nature always has its unique way of displaying the beauty of life. In an ancient garden in the south of our country, this natural cycle is perfectly embodied. Every spring, the garden is full of blooming spring lotuses, resembling pieces of emerald discs quietly floating on the surface of the water, attracting countless visitors to stop and admire. By autumn, the chrysanthemums outshine each other in beauty; yellow, purple, and white chrysanthemums sway in the autumn breeze, becoming a distinct scenic line in this ancient garden. All this seems to remind us that, no matter how the world changes, the beauty of nature is always worth cherishing and protecting.
FAITHFUL SIMPLE	[Global News Network] With the changing of seasons, nature always has its unique way to display the beauty of life. In an ancient garden in the south of our country, this natural cycle is perfectly embodied. Every spring, the garden is full of spring lotus, like pieces of green jade discs, quietly floating on the water surface, attracting countless visitors to stop and admire. And in autumn, it's the time for the autumn chrysanthemums to compete in beauty, with yellow, purple, and white chrysanthemums swaying in the autumn breeze, becoming a different landscape in this ancient garden. All of this seems to remind people that no matter how the world changes, the beauty of nature is always worth our appreciation and preservation.
CREATIVE SIMPLE	[Global News Network] As seasons transition, nature always has its unique way of showcasing the beauty of life. In an ancient garden in the southern part of our country, this natural cycle is perfectly embodied. Each spring, the garden blooms with lotus, like emerald discs quietly floating on the water, attracting countless visitors to stop and admire. Come autumn, it's a competition of chrysanthemums' beauty, with yellow, purple, and white chrysanthemums swaying in the autumn breeze, forming a distinctive landscape in this ancient garden. All these seem to remind us that, no matter how the world changes, the beauty of nature is always worth cherishing and protecting.
THEME SIMPLE	[Global News Network] With the change of seasons, Nature always has its unique way of showcasing the beauty of life. In an ancient garden in the southern part of our country, this natural cycle is perfectly represented. Every spring, the garden is full of blooming lotus, like pieces of emerald green jade plates quietly floating on the water, attracting countless visitors to stop and admire. And when autumn comes, it's time for the chrysanthemums to compete in beauty, with yellow, purple, and white chrysanthemums swaying in the autumn breeze, becoming a unique landscape of this ancient garden. All this seems to remind us that no matter how the world changes, the beauty of nature is always worth cherishing and protecting.
FAITHFUL COT	[Global News Network] As the seasons change, nature always has its unique way of showcasing the beauty of life. This natural cycle is perfectly embodied in an ancient garden in the southern part of our country. Every spring, the garden is filled with spring lotuses, which bloom like green jade discs quietly floating on the water, attracting countless visitors to stop and admire. When autumn arrives, it's the autumn chrysanthemums that compete in beauty, with yellow, purple, and white chrysanthemums swaying in the autumn breeze, forming a distinct landscape in this ancient garden. All of this seems to remind people that no matter how the world changes, the beauty of nature is always worth our appreciation and preservation.
CREATIVE COT	**Global News Network** - As seasons change, nature always finds its unique way to display the beauty of life. In an ancient garden in the south of our country, this natural cycle is perfectly exemplified. Every spring, the garden is adorned with lotus blossoms, like myriad verdant jade discs quietly floating on the water, drawing countless visitors to pause and admire. Come autumn, it's the chrysanthemums' turn to shine, with yellow, purple, and white blooms dancing in the autumn breeze, creating a distinct scenic line in this ancient garden. All these seem to remind us that, no matter how the world changes, the splendor of nature is always worth our appreciation and preservation.
THEME COT	[Global News Network] As the seasons change, nature always has its unique way of showcasing the beauty of life. In an ancient garden in the southern part of our country, this natural cycle is perfectly embodied. In spring, the garden is filled with blooming lotuses, like green jade plates quietly floating on the water, attracting countless visitors to stop and admire. In autumn, it's the chrysanthemums' turn to dazzle, with yellow, purple, and white blooms swaying in the autumn breeze, presenting a different kind of scenery in the ancient garden. All of this seems to remind us that no matter how the world changes, the beauty of nature is always worth cherishing and protecting.
FAITHFUL MULTI-TURN	[Global News Network] As the seasons change, nature always has its unique way of showcasing the beauty of life. In an ancient garden in the south of our country, this natural cycle is perfectly embodied. Each spring, the garden blooms with spring lotuses, like pieces of emerald green jade discs, quietly floating on the water's surface, attracting countless visitors to stop and admire. In autumn, it's the turn of the autumn chrysanthemums to compete in beauty, with yellow, purple, and white chrysanthemums swaying in the autumn breeze, becoming a distinctive landscape in this ancient garden. All of this seems to remind us that no matter how the world changes, the beauty of nature is always worth cherishing and preserving.
CREATIVE MULTI-TURN	[Global News Network] With the seasonal shifts, nature unfurls the splendor of life in its unique expressions. Within the verdant confines of an ancient garden in our country's south, this rhythmic cadence of nature is flawlessly manifested. Come spring, the garden is a spectacle of spring lotuses, mirroring a collection of emerald platters, serenely adrift upon the waters, luring myriad visitors to pause and revel in their beauty. Autumn heralds the reign of chrysanthemums, weaving a tapestry of yellow, purple, and white against the autumnal air, presenting a contrasting spectacle to the observer. Through this endless cycle of spring lotus and autumn chrysanthemum, nature subtly reminds us - amidst the ever-changing tapestry of life, its inherent beauty remains a constant, beckoning our appreciation and preservation.
THEME MULTI-TURN	[Global News Network] As the calendar pages turn, nature invariably reveals the splendor of existence in its distinct manner. In a venerable garden in the south of our nation, this perpetual dance of nature is exquisitely showcased. When spring arrives, the garden is awash with spring lotuses, resembling emerald plates, serenely floating on the water, enticing legions of visitors to halt and admire. Come autumn, the garden transitions to showcase the rival beauty of autumn chrysanthemums, with blooms of yellow, purple, and white swaying in the autumn breeze, crafting an alternative picturesque scene in this ancient park. This eternal sequence of lotus blossoms in spring and chrysanthemums in fall gently nudges us to remember that, despite the shifts and turns of worldly affairs, the beauty encapsulated within nature is always there, worthy of our protection and esteem.

Table 18: The example paragraph translations for plausible Chinese.

Method	Size	Chinese		Japanese		Korean		Plausible Chinese	
		Faithfulness	Creativity	Faithfulness	Creativity	Faithfulness	Creativity	Faithfulness	Creativity
GOOGLE	500	4.05 ± 0.76	3.43 ± 0.52	3.77 ± 0.96	3.43 ± 0.56	3.14 ± 1.00	3.15 ± 0.64	3.74 ± 0.86	3.59 ± 0.48
DEEPL	500	3.77 ± 1.00	3.46 ± 0.58	3.41 ± 1.06	3.40 ± 0.58	3.13 ± 1.01	3.38 ± 0.60	3.45 ± 1.00	3.66 ± 0.48
BASELINE	500	4.26 ± 0.59	3.70 ± 0.43	4.11 ± 0.73	3.63 ± 0.49	3.62 ± 0.83	3.46 ± 0.52	4.09 ± 0.67	3.84 ± 0.37
DIVERSITY EXPLICIT	2500	4.22 ± 0.53	3.86 ± 0.33	4.06 ± 0.63	3.78 ± 0.39	3.62 ± 0.77	3.68 ± 0.45	4.08 ± 0.57	3.95 ± 0.29
DIVERSITY DIALOG	2500	4.15 ± 0.51	3.94 ± 0.27	4.00 ± 0.59	3.87 ± 0.34	3.60 ± 0.75	3.79 ± 0.39	4.02 ± 0.55	4.02 ± 0.25
ZERO-SHOT CREATIVELY	500	4.30 ± 0.50	4.09 ± 0.23	4.16 ± 0.58	3.99 ± 0.27	3.76 ± 0.68	3.97 ± 0.33	4.21 ± 0.55	4.10 ± 0.28
CONTEXT EXPLICIT	2000	4.29 ± 0.58	3.73 ± 0.42	4.11 ± 0.70	3.62 ± 0.49	3.61 ± 0.81	3.48 ± 0.55	4.12 ± 0.65	3.86 ± 0.36
ANALOGY NATURAL	500	3.95 ± 0.70	4.06 ± 0.27	3.70 ± 0.74	4.03 ± 0.27	3.55 ± 0.72	3.97 ± 0.28	3.79 ± 0.78	4.06 ± 0.25
ANALOGY CREATIVE	500	3.19 ± 0.91	4.25 ± 0.31	3.07 ± 0.88	4.29 ± 0.32	2.80 ± 0.91	4.23 ± 0.35	3.10 ± 0.91	4.22 ± 0.29
SHUFFLE ORDER	500	4.29 ± 0.56	3.74 ± 0.40	4.16 ± 0.63	3.65 ± 0.47	3.65 ± 0.77	3.52 ± 0.49	4.14 ± 0.63	3.85 ± 0.36
SUCCINCT	500	4.21 ± 0.61	3.71 ± 0.44	4.10 ± 0.67	3.61 ± 0.49	3.66 ± 0.77	3.55 ± 0.48	4.05 ± 0.68	3.81 ± 0.38
TWO-STEP	500	3.89 ± 0.70	3.36 ± 0.57	3.68 ± 0.85	3.27 ± 0.57	3.26 ± 0.90	3.07 ± 0.61	3.71 ± 0.82	3.53 ± 0.52
DISCONTINUOUS 1	500	4.25 ± 0.60	3.74 ± 0.39	4.09 ± 0.67	3.63 ± 0.47	3.56 ± 0.85	3.59 ± 0.50	4.05 ± 0.68	3.84 ± 0.34
DISCONTINUOUS 2	500	4.13 ± 0.65	3.58 ± 0.49	3.95 ± 0.78	3.47 ± 0.53	3.44 ± 0.89	3.37 ± 0.60	3.90 ± 0.80	3.72 ± 0.44
FEW-SHOT	500	4.34 ± 0.53	3.86 ± 0.33	4.21 ± 0.65	3.79 ± 0.40	3.70 ± 0.77	3.72 ± 0.44	4.16 ± 0.59	3.93 ± 0.33
FEW-SHOT CREATIVELY	500	4.22 ± 0.61	4.08 ± 0.27	4.14 ± 0.64	4.05 ± 0.36	3.72 ± 0.71	4.01 ± 0.37	4.18 ± 0.56	4.08 ± 0.28

Table 19: The faithfulness and creativity scores for all strategies and all languages.

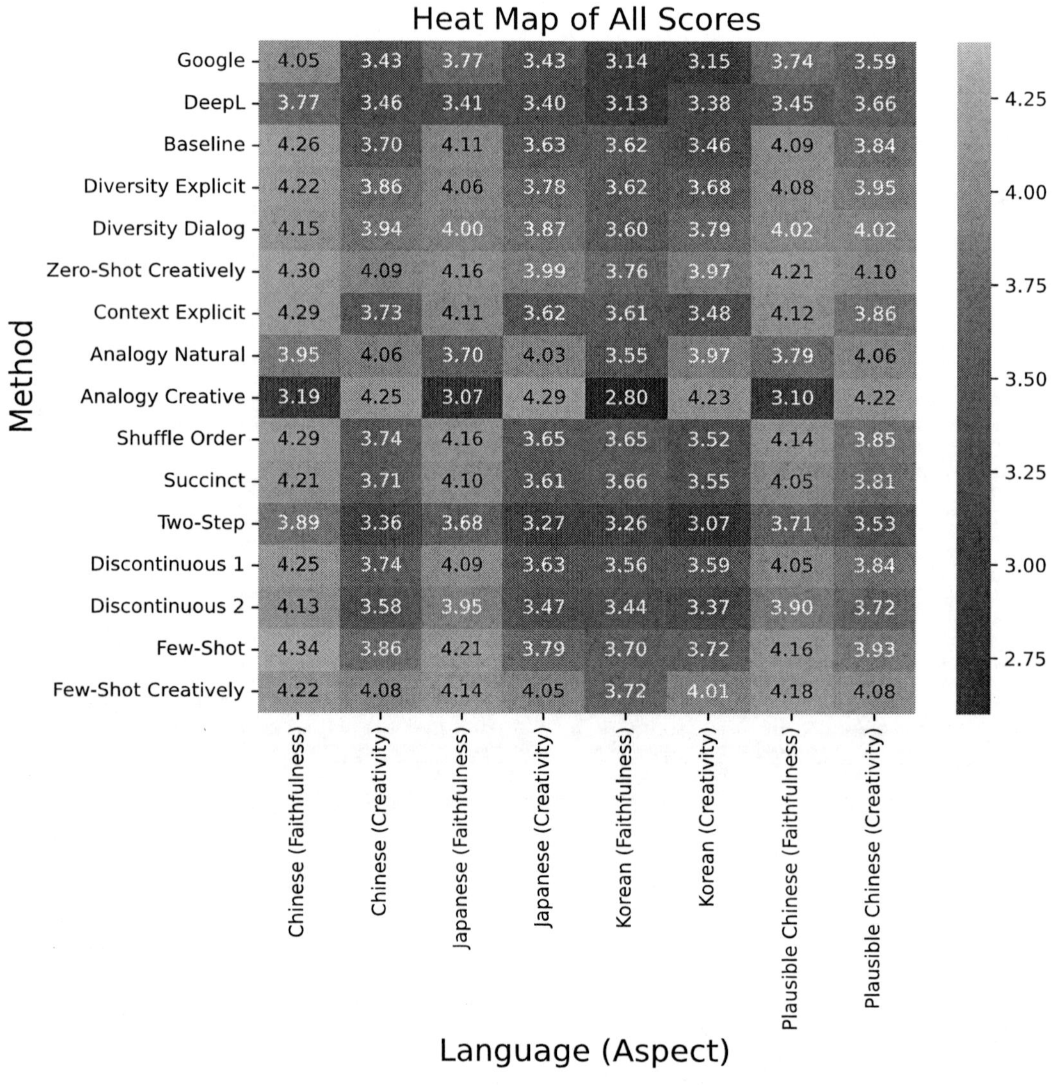

Figure 3: The heat map for all faithfulness and creativity scores.

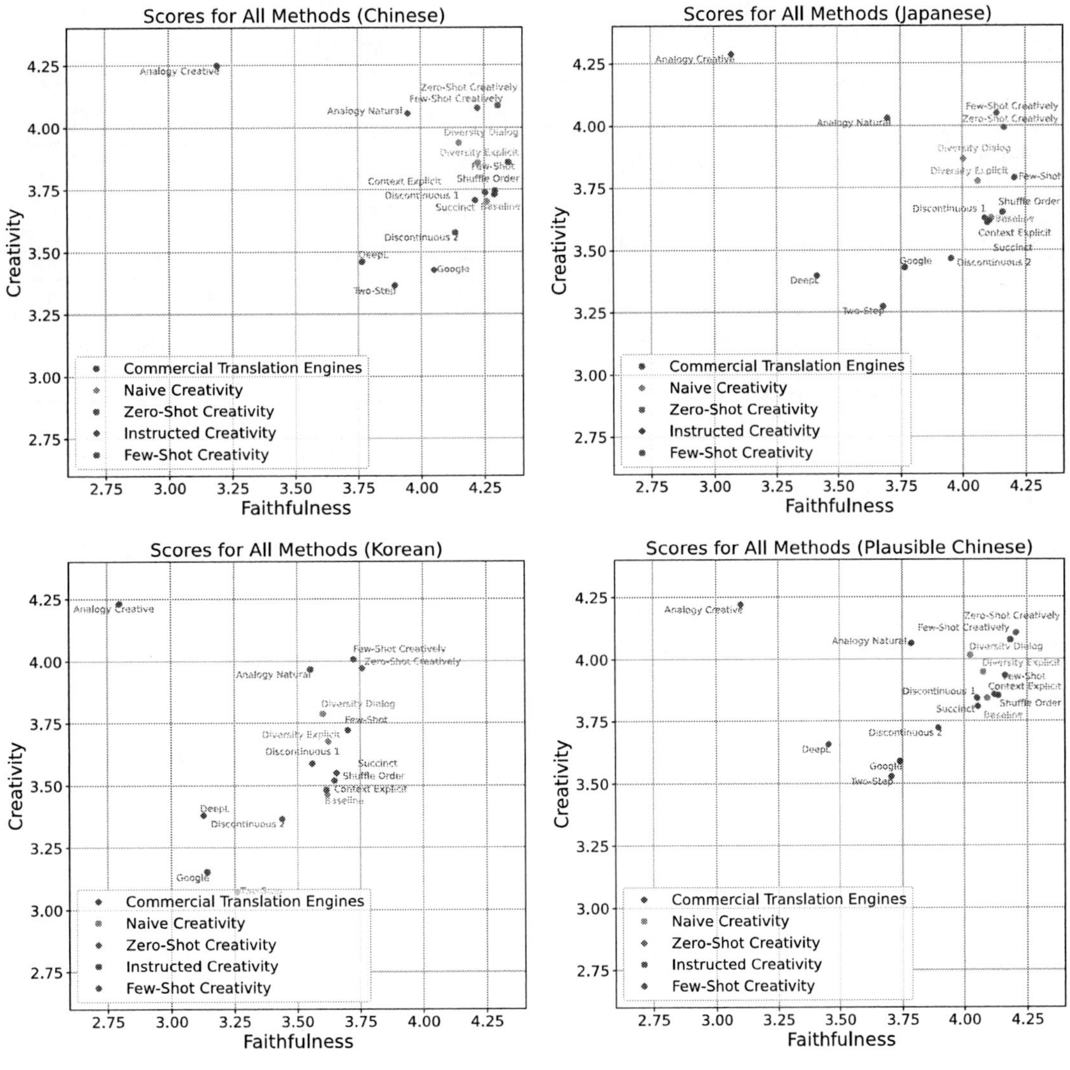

Figure 4: The scatter plots for all faithfulness and creativity scores.

An Empirical Study of Multilingual Vocabulary for Neural Machine Translation Models

Kenji Imamura and Masao Utiyama
National Institute of Information and Communications Technology,
Seika-cho, Kyoto, 619-0289, Japan
{kenji.imamura, mutiyama}@nict.go.jp

Abstract

In this paper, we discuss multilingual vocabulary for neural machine translation models. Multilingual vocabularies should generate highly accurate machine translations regardless of the languages, and have preferences so that tokenized strings contain rare out-of-vocabulary (OOV) tokens and token sequences are short. In this paper, we discuss the characteristics of various multilingual vocabularies via tokenization and translation experiments. We also present our recommended vocabulary and tokenizer.

1 Introduction

In recent tasks that use neural models, including neural machine translation, we usually fine-tune pretrained models (e.g., Devlin et al. (2019); Liu et al. (2020)). When a pretrained model is fine-tuned, the training corpora are different from those used for pretraining, in which the vocabulary must be different. However, pretrained models determine their vocabulary in advance, and it is difficult to change the vocabulary during fine-tuning. Therefore, it is important to discuss the first vocabulary.[1]

On the other hand, it becomes common to process multiple languages in machine translation and large language models (LLMs) because neural models can be packed multiple languages into a model (e.g., Johnson et al. (2017)). In this paper, we discuss vocabularies appropriate for multilingual neural models. The target task is machine translation that uses encoder-decoder models. Our aim is to decide the vocabulary that is suitable for our multilingual translation models.

Figure 1 illustrates the typical structure of an encoder-decoder model (Vaswani et al., 2017). In this structure, there are five modules related to vocabulary: 1) source tokenizer, 2) target tokenizer, 3) encoder embeddings, 4) decoder embeddings, and 5) output projector. The tokenizers tokenize a string into tokens, which consist of (sub-)words in the vocabulary of each tokenizer, except for out-of-vocabulary (OOV) strings. Neural models convert them into dense representations by looking up the tokens in the word embedding tables. Thus, the vocabularies in the tokenizers and neural model (the embedding tables and output projector) are essentially identical. It is possible to use different vocabularies between the encoder and decoder. However, shared vocabulary is generally used in multilingual models because both input and output strings are multilingual (e.g., Liu et al. (2020); Fan et al. (2020)). In this paper, we assume that the vocabularies of the above five modules are identical, unless otherwise specified.

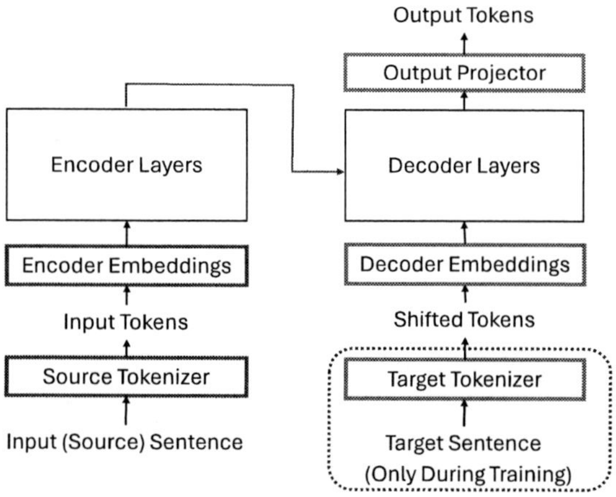

Figure 1: Vocabulary-related modules in an encoder-decoder model.

We suppose that the preferences or requirements of the multilingual vocabulary for neural models are as follows.

1. High accuracy is preferred in target tasks. Because we use the machine translation task in this paper, high translation quality is pre-

[1] It is possible to only add words in the vocabulary (Tang et al., 2020; Imamura and Sumita, 2022).

Proceedings of the Eleventh Workshop on Asian Translation (WAT 2024), pages 22–35
November 16, 2024 ©2024 Association for Computational Linguistics

ferred.

2. Token sequences, into which arbitrary strings are tokenized using the vocabulary, do not contain OOV tokens. This is a high preference because the OOV tokens certainly reduce the accuracy of tasks (Sennrich et al., 2016).

3. Token sequences are short (i.e., the numbers of tokens are small) because, generally, the shorter the input, the better the output (Arivazhagan et al., 2019).

4. Small models (i.e., the number of model parameters is small) are better for computation during training and inference. The number of parameters in the word embedding tables increases in proportion to the vocabulary size and accounts for a large portion in neural models. Therefore, a small vocabulary size is better from the viewpoint of the number of model parameters. However, it results in longer token sequences, and a tradeoff emerges between it and a preference for No. 3. We determine the balance of the two preferences using translation quality.

5. Regardless of the languages, strings with the same meaning are tokenized into similar numbers of tokens. We presume that this preference reduces complexity during translation.

6. The token sequences can be read by humans. Although this preference does not affect translation quality, high readability is better for debugging by humans.

In this paper, we discuss the vocabularies that satisfy the above preferences for multilingual models, which manage a mixture of various script types. Note that we consider No. 1 to be the most important preference, the second preference is No. 2, and the remaining preferences are optional.

The remainder of this paper is organized as follows: In Section 2, we explain related work, which includes studies of multilingual models. Next, we discuss preferred vocabulary via tokenization and translation experiments in Sections 3 and 4, respectively. In Section 5, we compare our experimental results with findings of conventional vocabulary studies, and we conclude the paper in Section 6.

2 Related Work

2.1 Multilingual Models

Table 1 shows the list of major multilingual (partially monolingual) models and their vocabularies/tokenizers.

Multilingual BERT (mBERT) (Devlin et al., 2019) and XLM-RoBERTa (XLM-R) (Conneau et al., 2020) are categorized as multilingual encoder models. These encoder models are applied to various natural language understanding tasks.

For encoder-decoder models, which are used for machine translation, multilingual BART (mBART) (Liu et al., 2020; Tang et al., 2020), M2M-100 (Fan et al., 2020), NLLB-200 (NLLB Team et al., 2022), and mT5 (Xue et al., 2021) are categorized as the multilingual models. Note that mBART and XLM-R use the same tokenization model.

Recent LLMs are resultantly multilingual, even though they learn using English Web text, because they contain other languages. Their vocabulary sizes are rather small: the size of GPT2 (Radford et al., 2019) is 50K and that of LlaMa2 (Touvron et al., 2023) is 32K.

Many multilingual models use SentencePiece (Kudo and Richardson, 2018) as their tokenizers. In this paper, we use SentencePiece for our experiments. Note that byte pair encoding (BPE) (Sennrich et al., 2016) and unigram models (Kudo, 2018) are known as major subword encoding methods. We use the unigram models in this paper.

2.2 Byte-level BPE / Byte Fallback

If an input string contains OOV characters, there are two behaviors of tokenizers (Table 2).

1) The tokenizer decomposes the OOV parts into characters. In this case, the word embeddings become unknown (indicated by `<UNK>`).

2) The tokenizer decomposes the OOV parts into byte sequences (Radford et al., 2019). This method is called byte-level BPE in the byte-pair encoding and byte fallback in SentencePiece. They assume that input strings are encoded in UTF-8. If the vocabulary of the neural models includes all bytes (256 bytes), no OOV tokens occur. However, readability decreases because humans cannot understand the string. Additionally, the decoder may generate invalid byte sequences that are

Type	Model	Tokenizer	#Langs.	Vocab. size	Byte fallback
Encoder only	mBERT	WordPiece (Schuster and Nakajima, 2012)	104	120K	
	XLM-R†	SentencePiece/Unigram (Kudo and Richardson, 2018)	100	250K	
Encoder-decoder	mBART†	SentencePiece/Unigram	100	250K	
	M2M-100	SentencePiece/BPE	100	128K	
	NLLB-200	SentencePiece/BPE	200	256K	
	mT5	SentencePiece/Unigram	101	250K	✓
Decoder only	GPT2	Byte-level BPE (Radford et al., 2019)	1	50K	✓
	LlaMa2	SentencePiece/BPE	1+‡	32K	✓

Table 1: Tokenizer and vocabulary of major multilingual models. †XLM-R and mBART use the same tokenizer with the same vocabulary. ‡ 90% of the training corpus of LlaMa2 is in English, and the rest is multilingual.

Method	Example
Source	群衆が集結しました。
1) Character	群␣<UNK>␣が␣集␣結␣しました␣。
2) Byte fallback	群␣<0xE8>␣<0xA1>␣<0x86>␣が␣集␣結␣しました␣。

Table 2: Example of byte fallback. Japanese character '衆' is fallbacked if it is not contained in the vocabulary.

not decoded into UTF-8 if byte fallback is applied to the decoder. The detokenizer must address this problem.

We also confirm the effects of byte fallback.

2.3 Flores+ Dataset

The Flores+ dataset (NLLB Team et al., 2022; Goyal et al., 2021)[2] is an evaluation dataset that covers 200 languages. It was created by translating sentences that were sampled from articles in English Wikinews, Wikijounior, and Wikivoyage into other languages. Therefore, the sentences are parallel among languages other than English. A total of 997 and 1,012 sentences are published as the development (dev) and development-test (devtest) sets, respectively.[3]

The dataset contains the language and its script type in the filenames. We use the categories (language names and script types) of Flores+ in this paper.

3 Tokenization Experiments

In this section, we evaluate tokenization using various vocabularies/tokenizers. We evaluate translation in Section 4.

3.1 Experimental Settings

Target Languages We selected 98 languages (26 script types) from the Flores+ dataset for which there were more than 100K lines in the CC-100 corpus (a set of monolingual corpora) (Conneau et al., 2020; Wenzek et al., 2020).

Considering the script types of Flores+, 55 out of 98 languages use a Latin script, such as English, and 20 languages use scripts unique to each language, such as Greek, (simplified and traditional) Chinese, Japanese, and Thai. The list of languages and script types is shown in Table 6 in Appendix A.

Tokenizer/vocabulary We evaluated M2M-100, XLM-R/mBART, NLLB-200, mT5, and LlaMa2 for existing models. For our original models, we evaluated unigram models of SentencePiece learned under various conditions.

Training Corpus for SentencePiece We randomly selected the training sets for each language from the CC-100 corpus.[4] We selected 20 million lines in total. The mean number of lines was approximately 200 thousand per language, but we controlled the sampling size using a temperature coefficient, as we describe later.

Other Settings for SentencePiece We used 0.9995 for character coverage, and the number of seed pieces was 100 times the vocabulary size.

Evaluation We evaluated the tokenization results of the 98 devtest sets in Flores+ using the following metrics.

[2] https://github.com/openlanguagedata/flores

[3] The test set is not published.

[4] The largest set in CC-100 is 1.8 billion lines of English and the smallest set is 120 thousand lines of Lingala.

- average number of tokens and variance (standard deviation) for all languages.
- total number of OOV tokens.
- number of fallbacked bytes when we applied byte fallback.

We preferred a small number of tokens (i.e., short token sequences) and a small number of OOV tokens. The low variance of the number of tokens indicated that sentences with the same meaning were tokenized in close number of tokens, regardless of the languages.

Comparison Methods We compared tokenizers/vocabularies under various conditions as follows.

- **Vocabulary Size:**
  We compared the vocabulary sizes 250K and 64K (or 100K). The vocabulary size affects the length of token sequences and neural model size.

- **Byte Fallback:**
  We compared cases with and without byte fallback. This condition influences the number of OOV tokens.

- **Additional Characters:**
  We added approximately 52K characters, which are U+0000 to U+D7FF in the basic multilingual plane of Unicode and have character names in the Python unicodedata module. Adding characters to the vocabulary enables us to control OOV tokens using an alternative to byte fallback.

  Note that we can also control OOV tokens by changing the character coverage setting during SentencePiece training. In this study, we used the additional character method to control OOV tokens.

- **Language Balance:**
  How to determine the sampling size of the training corpus for each language. We evaluated the following two methods, one is based on language distribution in the corpus, and another is based on the script types. The methods changed the importance of low-resource languages and languages that use the unique scripts. Both methods control the corpus size using the inverse temperature coefficient $1/\tau$ (temperature sampling) (Lample and Conneau, 2019; Arivazhagan et al., 2019).

  a) This case follows the distribution of the CC-100 corpus (hereafter, 'Corpus'). This means that the size of high-resource languages becomes large. The training corpus size s_l of language l is determined by the following equation.

  $$s_l \propto \left(\frac{c_l}{\sum_i^L c_i} \right)^{1/\tau}, \qquad (1)$$

  where c_l denotes the number of CC-100 lines of language l, and L denotes the number of languages ($= 98$).

  b) This case uses the script types (hereafter, 'Script'). The training size of each language is uniform for a script type. Smoothing is based on the number of languages in a script type. The size of the languages that use unique scripts becomes large and that of the languages using the Latin script becomes small even though we apply temperature sampling.

  $$s_l \propto \frac{(1/ns_l)^{1/\tau}}{\sum_i^L (1/ns_i)^{1/\tau}}, \qquad (2)$$

  where ns_l denotes the number of languages in the script type to which language l belongs (e.g., 55 languages belong to the Latin script type, and one language belongs to the Japanese script type).

3.2 Result 1: Language Balance

Before the comparison experiments, we determined the optimal inverse temperature coefficient $1/\tau$ by changing the training corpus size for SentencePiece. We evaluated the 250K vocabulary with byte fallback without additional characters.

Figure 2 shows the change of the number of tokens in the Flores+ devtest set when we changed the inverse temperature coefficient from 0.0 to 1.0. It includes the average of all languages, the average of the languages that use the unique script (20 languages; represented as 'Single' languages), and the average of the languages of the Latin script (55 languages; 'Latin' languages).

a) When we used the Corpus method, the number of tokens and the difference between the Single and Latin languages became the smallest when $1/\tau = 0.0$.

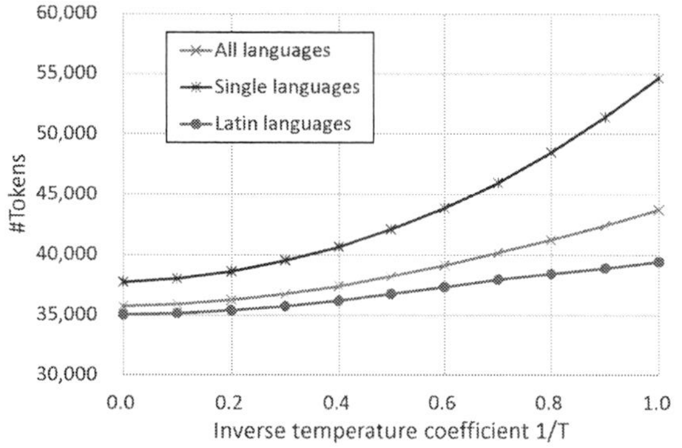

a) Corpus: Using the distribution of CC-100.

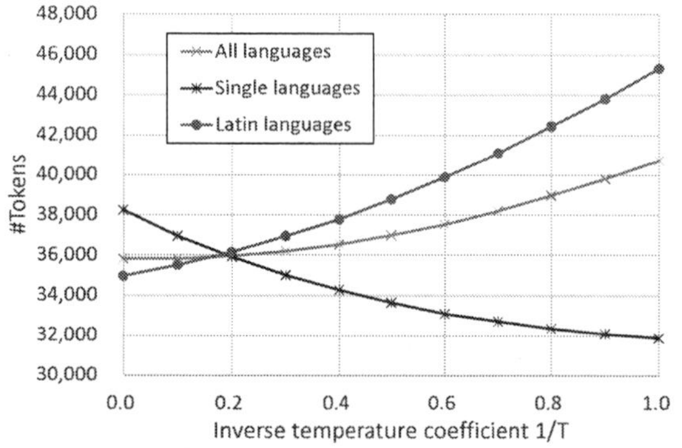

b) Script: Using the script types.

Figure 2: Number of tokens of Flores+ according to the inverse temperature coefficient $1/\tau$.

b) When we used the Script method, the number of tokens in the Latin languages increased as $1/\tau$ increased. Conversely, that of the Single languages decreased as $1/\tau$ increased and they were balanced when $1/\tau = 0.2$.

These results show that it was effective to balance languages by changing the training corpus size of each language using the inverse temperature coefficient. In subsequent experiments, we used the optimal inverse temperature coefficient that balanced all languages, that is, the standard deviation of the number of tokens became the smallest.

3.3 Result 2: Tokenization

Table 3 shows the tokenization results for the Flores+ devtest set using various tokenizers and vocabularies. 'Avg. #tokens' is the average number of tokens in all languages, and its standard deviation indicates the variance among languages. If the standard deviation is small, differences among languages must also be small. '#OOV' indicates the total number of OOV tokens, and '#Fallbacked bytes' is the total number of fallbacked bytes in all languages.

First, we confirmed the tokenization results of the baselines. The mBART/XLM-R and NLLB-200 tokenizers generated the least number of tokens, and mBART/XLM-R generated the least OOV tokens of the two tokenizers, even though it does not use byte fallback. From the viewpoint of OOV tokens, mT5, which uses byte fallback, was the best; however, the number of tokens was more than that of mBART/XLM-R. We consider that mBART/XLM-R was the most suitable tokenizer/vocabulary for our preferences (c.f., Section 1).

Next, we compared our SentencePiece unigram models, referring to the preferences. We confirm the translation quality in the next section.

First, the number of OOV tokens became zero using byte fallback.

The average number of tokens was most affected by the vocabulary size. The tokenizers with the 250K vocabulary became a similar number of tokens regardless of the other conditions. Although not shown in the table, the vocabulary size also affected the number of model parameters. When we used a Transformer big model (Vaswani et al., 2017), the number of model parameters was approximately 430 million for the 250K vocabulary and 240 million for the 64K vocabulary. The vocabulary size is a trade-off between the number of tokens and the number of parameters, and we determined the optimal size using translation quality.

The standard deviation of the number of tokens indicates the variance of languages. However, it was less affected by the language balance and byte fallback because all deviations of the 250K tokenizers were less than 3,700. It was most influenced by the size of the training corpus, as shown in Section 3.2.

Finally, focusing on the number of fallbacked bytes, the number decreased when there were additional characters. For example, 5,848 bytes in `250K_S+B` decreased to 48 bytes in `250K_S+B+C52K`. Adding characters is a solution to improve readability if translation quality is the same.

Tokenization examples of several languages are shown in Tables 8 to 10 in Appendix C.

Tokenizer/ vocabulary	Vocab. size	Byte fallback	Additional characters	Lang. balance	Avg. #tokens (std. dev.)	#OOV	# Fallbacked bytes
Baselines							
M2M-100	128K			Corpus	42,196 (8,542)	38,942	N/A
mBART/XLM-R	250K			Corpus	37,632 (6,246)	30	N/A
NLLB-200	256K			Corpus	37,579 (4,900)	16,739	N/A
mT5	250K	✓		Corpus	45,365 (9,979)	0	81
LlaMa2	32K	✓		–[5]	96,836 (75,630)	0	2,989,581
SentencePiece/Unigram							
250K_C+B	250K	✓	0	Corpus	35,562 (3,510)	0	11,601
250K_S	250K		0	Script	35,900 (3,422)	1,873	N/A
250K_S+B	250K	✓	0	Script	35,948 (3,367)	0	5,848
250K_S+B+C52K	250K	✓	52K	Script	37,095 (3,602)	0	48
64K_S+B	64K	✓	0	Script	45,504 (4,294)	0	4,745
100K_S+B+C52K	100K	✓	52K	Script	47,410 (4,676)	0	48

Table 3: Tokenization results. The tokenizer/vocabulary names of SentencePiece are combinations of the vocabulary size, language balance ('C' and 'S' represent 'Corpus' and 'Script,' respectively), byte fallback ('B'), and additional characters (C52K).

4 Translation Experiments

4.1 Experimental Settings

We evaluated the translation quality as follows:

Tokenizer/vocabulary From the tokenizers/vocabularies used in Section 3, we selected all SentencePiece vocabularies and mBART/XLM-R and mT5 as the baselines.

Translation Languages We selected the following eight out of 98 languages and trained a multilingual translation model in all directions ($8 \times 7 = 56$ directions) for each vocabulary:

- **Latin Languages:**
  English, Spanish, and Vietnamese: We selected one European language and one Asian language other than English.
- **Single Languages:**
  Japanese and Mandarin Chinese (Standard Beijing): Although their characters have the same origin, they use different glyphs (i.e., different character codes), in most cases.
- **Other Languages:**
  Modern Standard Arabic, Hindi, and Russian: These are the other script types of the above languages.

Parallel Corpus We sampled 1 million sentences for each language pair from the NLLB-200 corpus as the parallel corpus to train the translation models. We sampled sentences independently for each language pair. Therefore, the importances of the languages are the same in this experiment.

Translation Models We used the Transformer big models (Vaswani et al., 2017) (1,024 embedding and 4,096 FFN dimensions, six layers for the encoder and decoder) implemented by FairSeq (Ott et al., 2019), and learned multilingual models in 56 (8×7) directions. Like the M2M-100 model (Fan et al., 2020), the multilingual models were trained while we supplied language tags (e.g., '`__en__`' for English) at the head of the source and target sentences.

Hyperparameters The details of the hyperparameters are shown in Appendix B.

Evaluation We evaluated the translation quality using the average scores of 56 directions of ChrF++ (Popović, 2017) and COMET (Rei et al., 2022) (using the `wmt22-comet-da` model) implemented in SacreBLEU (Post, 2018). For the statistical test, we used binomial testing with 56 trials, in which a trial indicated a direction ($p < 0.05$).

4.2 Results

Table 4 shows the translation quality for each vocabulary. Among all vocabularies, mBART/XLM-R achieved the highest scores. This is because it contained (not zero, but) very few OOV tokens and the number of tokens was low.

Next, we focused on the results of our SentencePiece unigram models. Regarding the vocabulary size, the translation qualities of the 250K

[5]This vocabulary does not balance languages because the model is not precisely multilingual.

Tokenizer/vocabulary	Vocab. size	Byte fallback	Additional characters	Lang. balance	Avg. score ChrF++	Avg. score COMET
Baselines						
XLM-R/mBART	250K			Corpus	**41.13**	**.8237**
mT5	250K	√		Corpus	40.44	.8176
SentencePiece/Unigram						
250K_C+B	250K	√	0	Corpus	<u>40.93</u>	.8211
250K_S	250K		0	Script	40.72	.8167
250K_S+B	250K	√	0	Script	<u>40.93</u>	<u>.8212</u>
250K_S+B+C52K	250K	√	52K	Script	40.89	.8208
64K_S+B	64K	√	0	Script	40.21	.8139
100K_S+B+C52K	100K	√	52K	Script	40.09	.8127

Table 4: Translation quality for each tokenizer/vocabulary. The tokenizer/vocabulary names of SentencePiece consisted of the vocabulary size, language balance ('C' is Corpus, and 'S' is Script Type), byte fallback (B), and additional characters (C52K). The bold scores indicate the highest score, and the underlined scores indicate the second-best scores.

vocabularies were better than those of the 64k (or 100K) sizes. For example, the ChrF++ and COMET scores of `250K_S+B` were higher than those of `64K_S+B` ($p = 1.6 \times 10^{-15}$), and the scores of `250K_S+B+C52K` were higher than those of `100K_S+B+C52K` ($p = 5.6 \times 10^{-17}$).

The translation quality with byte fallback was significantly higher than that without byte fallback when comparing `250K_S` and `250K_S+B` ($p = 2.5 \times 10^{-5}$), even though the difference was small.

Regarding additional characters, although we could not find a significant difference between `250K_S+B` and `250K_S+B+C52K`, the scores of `64K_S+B` were significantly higher than those of `100K_S+B+C52K` ($p = 6.1 \times 10^{-4}$). Additional characters were not effective. We suppose that this was because multi-character subwords reduced in the vocabulary or characters that were not learned remained when we added 52K characters.

4.3 When Different Vocabulary Sizes are Used between the Encoder and Decoder

In the preceding discussion, we assumed that a shared vocabulary was used in the encoder and decoder. However, the optimal vocabularies of the encoder and decoder may not be the same because the encoder is responsible for natural language understanding, and the decoder is responsible for generation. Therefore, in this subsection, we confirm the translation quality if we change the vocabulary between the encoder and decoder.

Specifically, we performed a translation experiment by changing the vocabulary sizes between the encoder and decoder. We used `250K_S+B` and `64K_S+B` (i.e., the language balance was the script type, with byte fallback, and the vocabulary sizes were 250K and 64K).

Vocab. size Encoder	Vocab. size Decoder	ChrF++	COMET
250K	250K	**40.93**	**.8212**
250K	64K	40.73	.8192
64K	250K	40.82	.8203
64K	64K	40.21	.8139

Table 5: Translation quality (average scores in the 56 directions) when changing the vocabulary sizes of the encoder and decoder.

Table 5 shows the result. Regardless of whether we changed the vocabulary size of the encoder or decoder, the scores were intermediate between those of 250K and 64K. The shared vocabulary of the encoder and decoder was suitable to achieve high translation quality.

5 Comparison with Conventional Vocabulary Studies

There have been various vocabulary studies using multilingual neural models. The findings of these studies, in comparison with the results of our study, can be summarized as follows:

Arivazhagan et al. (2019) built multilingual models covering 103 languages using various conditions. They also investigated vocabularies for the models and reported the following findings.

1. Translation quality is better when a large vocabulary is used.
2. Changes to the language balance of the vocabulary using temperature sampling do not

significantly affect translation quality.

In our experiments, a large vocabulary resulted in better translation quality. In addition, the language balance was not observed to have a significant effect on quality.

Gowda and May (2020) investigated the optimal vocabulary size for multiple languages (using only single-directional translation models). They reported that the optimal vocabulary size depends on the training corpus size for the translation models. Namely, a large vocabulary is better in high-resource languages and a small vocabulary is preferable low-resource languages. As described in Section 4, our experiments indicate that a large vocabulary is better because we use 1,000,000 parallel sentences for each direction, which is regarded as a high-resource condition.

Zhang et al. (2022) constructed multilingual vocabularies for eight languages with different English ratios in the training corpora, and investigated the impact on the translation quality. In addition to the findings of conventional studies, they investigated the effects of byte fallback and showed that this feature does not significantly affect the translation quality. In our experiments, in addition to eliminating OOV tokens, byte fallback was found to enhance the translation quality. Therefore, we consider it preferable to use byte fallback.

6 Conclusions

In this paper, we discussed multilingual vocabulary for neural machine translation models. Our findings are summarized as follows:

1. Among all vocabularies, mBART/XLM-R was the best in the machine translation task. Although the tokenizer of mBART/XLM-R did not use byte fallback, the number of OOV tokens was small and, consequently, the translation quality became high.

   Among the vocabularies of our SentencePiece models, the vocabularies of 250K with byte fallback achieved high quality.

2. Byte fallback was effective for eliminating OOV tokens, and the translation quality was better than that without byte fallback.

3. The vocabularies of the 250K size generated the smallest number of tokens (the shortest length of token sequences). These vocabularies had the disadvantage that the number of model parameters increased. However, translation quality was better than that for the 64K vocabulary.

4. To tokenize multilingual sentences into a similar (close) number of tokens, it was effective to control the training data size of each language. It could be controlled using a temperature coefficient.

5. Readability increased when the number of fallbacked bytes was low. However, translation quality decreased when we increased character coverage by adding characters into the vocabulary.

Recommended Vocabulary/Tokenizer Based on the vocabulary of mBART/XLM-R, we recommend using a tokenizer with byte fallback. In future work, we will build multilingual translation models using the multilingual vocabulary discussed in this paper.

Limitations

The results in this paper were a case study because our experiments were not comprehensive.

Ethics Statement

Our vocabularies were created automatically from corpora, and we did not check the contents. Therefore, they may contain inappropriate words.

Acknowledgments

Part of this work was conducted under the commissioned research program 'Research and Development of Advanced Multilingual Translation Technology' in the 'R&D Project for Information and Communications Technology (JPMI00316)' of the Ministry of Internal Affairs and Communications (MIC), Japan.

References

Naveen Arivazhagan, Ankur Bapna, Orhan Firat, Dmitry Lepikhin, Melvin Johnson, Maxim Krikun, Mia Xu Chen, Yuan Cao, George Foster, Colin Cherry, Wolfgang Macherey, Zhifeng Chen, and Yonghui Wu. 2019. Massively multilingual neural machine translation in the wild: Findings and challenges. *Preprint*, arXiv:1907.05019.

Alexis Conneau, Kartikay Khandelwal, Naman Goyal, Vishrav Chaudhary, Guillaume Wenzek, Francisco Guzmán, Edouard Grave, Myle Ott, Luke Zettlemoyer, and Veselin Stoyanov. 2020. Unsupervised cross-lingual representation learning at scale. In *Proceedings of the 58th Annual Meeting of the Association for Computational Linguistics*, pages 8440–8451, Online. Association for Computational Linguistics.

Jacob Devlin, Ming-Wei Chang, Kenton Lee, and Kristina Toutanova. 2019. BERT: Pre-training of deep bidirectional transformers for language understanding. In *Proceedings of the 2019 Conference of the North American Chapter of the Association for Computational Linguistics: Human Language Technologies, Volume 1 (Long and Short Papers)*, pages 4171–4186, Minneapolis, Minnesota. Association for Computational Linguistics.

Angela Fan, Shruti Bhosale, Holger Schwenk, Zhiyi Ma, Ahmed El-Kishky, Siddharth Goyal, Mandeep Baines, Onur Celebi, Guillaume Wenzek, Vishrav Chaudhary, Naman Goyal, Tom Birch, Vitaliy Liptchinsky, Sergey Edunov, Edouard Grave, Michael Auli, and Armand Joulin. 2020. Beyond english-centric multilingual machine translation. *arXiv e-print*, 2010.11125. *arXiv preprint*.

Thamme Gowda and Jonathan May. 2020. Finding the optimal vocabulary size for neural machine translation. In *Findings of the Association for Computational Linguistics: EMNLP 2020*, pages 3955–3964, Online. Association for Computational Linguistics.

Naman Goyal, Cynthia Gao, Vishrav Chaudhary, Peng-Jen Chen, Guillaume Wenzek, Da Ju, Sanjana Krishnan, Marc'Aurelio Ranzato, Francisco Guzmán, and Angela Fan. 2021. The flores-101 evaluation benchmark for low-resource and multilingual machine translation.

Kenji Imamura and Eiichiro Sumita. 2022. Extending the subwording model of multilingual pretrained models for new languages. *Preprint*, arXiv:2211.15965.

Melvin Johnson, Mike Schuster, Quoc V. Le, Maxim Krikun, Yonghui Wu, Zhifeng Chen, Nikhil Thorat, Fernanda Viégas, Martin Wattenberg, Greg Corrado, Macduff Hughes, and Jeffrey Dean. 2017. Google's multilingual neural machine translation system: Enabling zero-shot translation. *Transactions of the Association for Computational Linguistics*, 5:339–351.

Taku Kudo. 2018. Subword regularization: Improving neural network translation models with multiple subword candidates. In *Proceedings of the 56th Annual Meeting of the Association for Computational Linguistics (Volume 1: Long Papers)*, pages 66–75, Melbourne, Australia. Association for Computational Linguistics.

Taku Kudo and John Richardson. 2018. SentencePiece: A simple and language independent subword tokenizer and detokenizer for neural text processing. In *Proceedings of the 2018 Conference on Empirical Methods in Natural Language Processing: System Demonstrations*, pages 66–71, Brussels, Belgium. Association for Computational Linguistics.

Guillaume Lample and Alexis Conneau. 2019. Cross-lingual language model pretraining. In *Proceedings of the 33rd International Conference on Neural Information Processing Systems (NIPS-2019)*, pages 7059–7069.

Yinhan Liu, Jiatao Gu, Naman Goyal, Xian Li, Sergey Edunov, Marjan Ghazvininejad, Mike Lewis, and Luke Zettlemoyer. 2020. Multilingual denoising pre-training for neural machine translation. *Transactions of the Association for Computational Linguistics*, 8:726–742.

NLLB Team, Marta R. Costa-jussà, James Cross, Onur Çelebi, Maha Elbayad, Kenneth Heafield, Kevin Heffernan, Elahe Kalbassi, Janice Lam, Daniel Licht, Jean Maillard, Anna Sun, Skyler Wang, Guillaume Wenzek, Al Youngblood, Bapi Akula, Loic Barrault, Gabriel Mejia Gonzalez, Prangthip Hansanti, John Hoffman, Semarley Jarrett, Kaushik Ram Sadagopan, Dirk Rowe, Shannon Spruit, Chau Tran, Pierre Andrews, Necip Fazil Ayan, Shruti Bhosale, Sergey Edunov, Angela Fan, Cynthia Gao, Vedanuj Goswami, Francisco Guzmán, Philipp Koehn, Alexandre Mourachko, Christophe Ropers, Safiyyah Saleem, Holger Schwenk, and Jeff Wang. 2022. No language left behind: Scaling human-centered machine translation. *arXiv e-print*, 2207.04672. *Preprint*, arXiv:2207.04672.

Myle Ott, Sergey Edunov, Alexei Baevski, Angela Fan, Sam Gross, Nathan Ng, David Grangier, and Michael Auli. 2019. fairseq: A fast, extensible toolkit for sequence modeling. In *Proceedings of the 2019 Conference of the North American Chapter of the Association for Computational Linguistics (Demonstrations)*, pages 48–53, Minneapolis, Minnesota. Association for Computational Linguistics.

Maja Popović. 2017. chrF++: words helping character n-grams. In *Proceedings of the Second Conference on Machine Translation*, pages 612–618, Copenhagen, Denmark. Association for Computational Linguistics.

Matt Post. 2018. A call for clarity in reporting BLEU scores. In *Proceedings of the Third Conference on Machine Translation: Research Papers*, pages 186–191, Brussels, Belgium. Association for Computational Linguistics.

Alec Radford, Jeff Wu, Rewon Child, David Luan, Dario Amodei, and Ilya Sutskever. 2019. Language models are unsupervised multitask learners.

Ricardo Rei, José G. C. de Souza, Duarte Alves, Chrysoula Zerva, Ana C Farinha, Taisiya Glushkova, Alon Lavie, Luisa Coheur, and André

F. T. Martins. 2022. COMET-22: Unbabel-IST 2022 submission for the metrics shared task. In *Proceedings of the Seventh Conference on Machine Translation (WMT)*, pages 578–585, Abu Dhabi, United Arab Emirates (Hybrid). Association for Computational Linguistics.

Mike Schuster and Kaisuke Nakajima. 2012. Japanese and Korean voice search. In *IEEE International Conference on Acoustics, Speech and Signal Processing*.

Rico Sennrich, Barry Haddow, and Alexandra Birch. 2016. Neural machine translation of rare words with subword units. In *Proceedings of the 54th Annual Meeting of the Association for Computational Linguistics (Volume 1: Long Papers)*, pages 1715–1725, Berlin, Germany. Association for Computational Linguistics.

Yuqing Tang, Chau Tran, Xian Li, Peng-Jen Chen, Naman Goyal, Vishrav Chaudhary, Jiatao Gu, and Angela Fan. 2020. Multilingual translation with extensible multilingual pretraining and finetuning. *arXiv e-print*, 2008.00401. *Preprint*, arXiv:2008.00401.

Hugo Touvron, Louis Martin, Kevin Stone, Peter Albert, Amjad Almahairi, Yasmine Babaei, Nikolay Bashlykov, Soumya Batra, Prajjwal Bhargava, Shruti Bhosale, Dan Bikel, Lukas Blecher, Cristian Canton Ferrer, Moya Chen, Guillem Cucurull, David Esiobu, Jude Fernandes, Jeremy Fu, Wenyin Fu, Brian Fuller, Cynthia Gao, Vedanuj Goswami, Naman Goyal, Anthony Hartshorn, Saghar Hosseini, Rui Hou, Hakan Inan, Marcin Kardas, Viktor Kerkez, Madian Khabsa, Isabel Kloumann, Artem Korenev, Punit Singh Koura, Marie-Anne Lachaux, Thibaut Lavril, Jenya Lee, Diana Liskovich, Yinghai Lu, Yuning Mao, Xavier Martinet, Todor Mihaylov, Pushkar Mishra, Igor Molybog, Yixin Nie, Andrew Poulton, Jeremy Reizenstein, Rashi Rungta, Kalyan Saladi, Alan Schelten, Ruan Silva, Eric Michael Smith, Ranjan Subramanian, Xiaoqing Ellen Tan, Binh Tang, Ross Taylor, Adina Williams, Jian Xiang Kuan, Puxin Xu, Zheng Yan, Iliyan Zarov, Yuchen Zhang, Angela Fan, Melanie Kambadur, Sharan Narang, Aurelien Rodriguez, Robert Stojnic, Sergey Edunov, and Thomas Scialom. 2023. Llama 2: Open foundation and fine-tuned chat models. *Preprint*, arXiv:2307.09288.

Ashish Vaswani, Noam Shazeer, Niki Parmar, Jakob Uszkoreit, Llion Jones, Aidan N. Gomez, Lukasz Kaiser, and Illia Polosukhin. 2017. Attention is all you need. *CoRR*, abs/1706.03762.

Guillaume Wenzek, Marie-Anne Lachaux, Alexis Conneau, Vishrav Chaudhary, Francisco Guzmán, Armand Joulin, and Edouard Grave. 2020. CCNet: Extracting high quality monolingual datasets from web crawl data. In *Proceedings of the Twelfth Language Resources and Evaluation Conference*, pages 4003–4012, Marseille, France. European Language Resources Association.

Linting Xue, Noah Constant, Adam Roberts, Mihir Kale, Rami Al-Rfou, Aditya Siddhant, Aditya Barua, and Colin Raffel. 2021. mT5: A massively multilingual pre-trained text-to-text transformer. In *Proceedings of the 2021 Conference of the North American Chapter of the Association for Computational Linguistics: Human Language Technologies*, pages 483–498, Online. Association for Computational Linguistics.

Shiyue Zhang, Vishrav Chaudhary, Naman Goyal, James Cross, Guillaume Wenzek, Mohit Bansal, and Francisco Guzman. 2022. How robust is neural machine translation to language imbalance in multilingual tokenizer training? In *Proceedings of the 15th biennial conference of the Association for Machine Translation in the Americas (Volume 1: Research Track)*, pages 97–116, Orlando, USA. Association for Machine Translation in the Americas.

A Language List in this Paper

Table 6 shows the list of 98 languages used in this paper, which is organized by script type.

B Hyperparameters for Translation Experiments

Table 7 shows the list of hyperparameters used in the experiments in Section 4.

C Tokenization Examples

Tables 8 to 10 show tokenization examples, in which the same sentences (or translations) obtained from the Flores+ dev set were tokenized by each tokenizer. Depending on the tokenizers, the number of tokens vary significantly in a language, and each tokenizer has strong and weak languages. Among the tokenizers, `mBART/XLM-R` and `250K_S+B` tokenized the sentences into fewer tokens on average.

Script type	#Langs.	Languages
Arabic	6	**Modern Standard Arabic**, Southern Pashto, Western Persian, Sindhi, Urdu, Uyghur
Armenian	1	Armenian
Bengali	2	Assamese, Bengali
Cyrillic	9	Belarusian, Bulgarian, Kazakh, Kyrgyz, Macedonian, Halh Mongolian, **Russian**, Serbian, Ukrainian
Devanagari	4	**Hindi**, Marathi, Nepali, Sanskrit
Ge'ez	1	Amharic
Georgian	1	Georgian
Greek	1	Greek
Gujarati	1	Gujarati
Gurmukhi	1	Eastern Panjabi
Hebrew	2	Hebrew, Eastern Yiddish
Hungul	1	Korean
Japanese	1	**Japanese**
Kannada	1	Kannada
Khmer	1	Khmer
Lao	1	Lao
Latin	55	Afrikaans, Tosk Albanian, North Azerbaijani, Basque, Norwegian Bokmål, Bosnian, Catalan, Haitian Creole, Croatian, Czech, Danish, Dutch, **English**, Esperanto, Estonian, Finnish, French, Scottish Gaelic, Galician, Ganda, German, Hausa, Hungarian, Icelandic, Igbo, Indonesian, Irish, Italian, Javanese, Northern Kurdish, Standard Latvian, Lingala, Lithuanian, Plateau Malagasy, Standard Malay, West Central Oromo, Polish, Portuguese, Romanian, Slovak, Slovenian, Somali, **Spanish**, Sundanese, Swahili, Swedish, Tagalog / Filipino, Tswana, Turkish, Northern Uzbek, **Vietnamese**, Welsh, Wolof, Xhosa, Zulu
Malayalam	1	Malayalam
Myanmar	1	Burmese
Odia	1	Odia
Simplified Chinese	1	**Mandarin Chinese (Standard Beijing)**
Sinhala	1	Sinhala
Tamil	1	Tamil
Telugu	1	Telugu
Thai	1	Thai
Traditional Chinese	1	Mandarin Chinese (Taiwanese)
Total	98	

Table 6: Script types and languages. #Langs. indicates the number of languages. The languages in bold were used in the translation experiments.

Type	Name	Setting
Model	Architecture	Transformer big
	Embedding dimension	1,024
	FFN inner dimension	4,096
Training	Dropout	0.3
	Loss function	Label smoothed cross-entropy
	Label smoothing	$\epsilon = 0.1$
	Optimizer	Adam ($\beta_1 = 0.9$, $\beta_2 = 0.98$)
	Learning rate	5e-4
	LR scheduler	Inverse square root
	Warm-up steps	4,000
	Global batch size	Roughly 128,000 tokens
	Early Stopping	No-update 9 epochs
Test	Beam width	10

Table 7: Hyperparameters for the translation experiments.

Tokenizer/ vocabulary	English #Tokens	English Sample	Spanish #Tokens	Spanish Sample	Vietnamese #Tokens	Vietnamese Sample
M2M-100	15	▁Local ⊔ ▁media ⊔ ▁reports ⊔ ▁an ⊔ ▁air ⊔ port ⊔ ▁fire ⊔ ▁vehicle ⊔ ▁roll ⊔ ed ⊔ ▁over ⊔ ▁while ⊔ ▁respond ⊔ ing ⊔ .	23	▁La ⊔ ▁prensa ⊔ ▁local ⊔ ▁inform ⊔ ó ⊔ ▁que ⊔ ▁una ⊔ ▁patr ⊔ ulla ⊔ ▁de ⊔ ▁bom ⊔ ber ⊔ os ⊔ ▁del ⊔ ▁aerop ⊔ uerto ⊔ ▁vol ⊔ có ⊔ ▁mientras ⊔ ▁presta ⊔ ba ⊔ ▁servicio ⊔ .	19	▁Truyền ⊔ ▁thông ⊔ ▁địa ⊔ ▁phương ⊔ ▁đưa ⊔ ▁tin ⊔ ▁một ⊔ ▁phương ⊔ ▁tiện ⊔ ▁chữa ⊔ ▁cháy ⊔ ▁sân ⊔ ▁bay ⊔ ▁đã ⊔ ▁tới ⊔ ▁khi ⊔ ▁trả ⊔ ▁lời ⊔ .
mBART/XLM-R	14	▁Local ⊔ ▁media ⊔ ▁reports ⊔ ▁an ⊔ ▁airport ⊔ ▁fire ⊔ ▁vehicle ⊔ ▁rolle ⊔ d ⊔ ▁over ⊔ ▁while ⊔ ▁respond ⊔ ing ⊔ .	20	▁La ⊔ ▁prensa ⊔ ▁local ⊔ ▁inform ó ⊔ ▁que ⊔ ▁una ⊔ ▁patru ⊔ lla ⊔ ▁de ⊔ ▁bombe ⊔ ros ⊔ ▁del ⊔ ▁aeropuerto ⊔ ▁vol ⊔ có ⊔ ▁mientras ⊔ ▁presta ⊔ ba ⊔ ▁servicio ⊔ .	19	▁Truyền ⊔ ▁thông ⊔ ▁địa ⊔ ▁phương ⊔ ▁đưa ⊔ ▁tin ⊔ ▁một ⊔ ▁phương ⊔ ▁tiện ⊔ ▁chữa ⊔ ▁cháy ⊔ ▁sân ⊔ ▁bay ⊔ ▁đã ⊔ ▁tới ⊔ ▁khi ⊔ ▁trả ⊔ ▁lời ⊔ .
NLLB-200	14	▁Local ⊔ ▁media ⊔ ▁reports ⊔ ▁an ⊔ ▁airport ⊔ ▁fire ⊔ ▁vehicle ⊔ ▁rol ⊔ led ⊔ ▁over ⊔ ▁while ⊔ ▁respond ⊔ ing ⊔ .	22	▁La ⊔ ▁prensa ⊔ ▁local ⊔ ▁inform ⊔ ó ⊔ ▁que ⊔ ▁una ⊔ ▁patr ⊔ ulla ⊔ ▁de ⊔ ▁bom ⊔ beros ⊔ ▁del ⊔ ▁aerop ⊔ uerto ⊔ ▁vol ⊔ có ⊔ ▁mientras ⊔ ▁presta ⊔ ba ⊔ ▁servicio ⊔ .	20	▁Tru ⊔ yền ⊔ ▁thông ⊔ ▁địa ⊔ ▁phương ⊔ ▁đưa ⊔ ▁tin ⊔ ▁một ⊔ ▁phương ⊔ ▁tiện ⊔ ▁chữa ⊔ ▁cháy ⊔ ▁sân ⊔ ▁bay ⊔ ▁đã ⊔ ▁tới ⊔ ▁khi ⊔ ▁trả ⊔ ▁lời ⊔ .
mT5	16	▁Local ⊔ ▁media ⊔ ▁ ⊔ reports ⊔ ▁an ⊔ ▁airport ⊔ ▁fire ⊔ ▁vehicle ⊔ ▁ ⊔ rolled ⊔ ▁over ⊔ ▁ ⊔ while ⊔ ▁respond ⊔ ing ⊔ .	25	▁La ⊔ ▁ ⊔ prensa ⊔ ▁local ⊔ ▁inform ⊔ ó ⊔ ▁que ⊔ ▁una ⊔ ▁patrul ⊔ la ⊔ ▁de ⊔ ▁ ⊔ bomber ⊔ os ⊔ ▁del ⊔ ▁aero ⊔ puerto ⊔ ▁vol ⊔ có ⊔ ▁mi ⊔ entras ⊔ ▁presta ⊔ ba ⊔ ▁servicio ⊔ .	38	▁Tr ⊔ uyền ⊔ ▁th ⊔ ông ⊔ ▁đ ⊔ ịa ⊔ ▁p ⊔ hương ⊔ ▁đư ⊔ a ⊔ ▁tin ⊔ ▁m ⊔ ột ⊔ ▁p ⊔ hương ⊔ ▁ ⊔ t ⊔ iện ⊔ ▁ch ⊔ ữ ⊔ a ⊔ ▁chá ⊔ y ⊔ ▁ ⊔ sân ⊔ ▁bay ⊔ ▁đ ⊔ ã ⊔ ▁ ⊔ t ⊔ ới ⊔ ▁khi ⊔ ▁tr ⊔ ả ⊔ ▁ ⊔ l ⊔ ời ⊔ .
LlaMa2	14	▁Local ⊔ ▁media ⊔ ▁reports ⊔ ▁an ⊔ ▁air ⊔ port ⊔ ▁fire ⊔ ▁vehicle ⊔ ▁rolled ⊔ ▁over ⊔ ▁while ⊔ ▁respond ⊔ ing ⊔ .	27	▁La ⊔ ▁pr ⊔ ensa ⊔ ▁local ⊔ ▁inform ⊔ ó ⊔ ▁que ⊔ ▁una ⊔ ▁patr ⊔ ulla ⊔ ▁de ⊔ ▁bom ⊔ ber ⊔ os ⊔ ▁del ⊔ ▁aer ⊔ op ⊔ uerto ⊔ ▁vol ⊔ c ⊔ ó ⊔ ▁mientras ⊔ ▁prest ⊔ aba ⊔ ▁serv ⊔ icio ⊔ .	53	▁Tru ⊔ y ⊔ ề ⊔ n ⊔ ▁th ⊔ ô ⊔ ng ⊔ ▁ ⊔ đ ⊔ ị ⊔ a ⊔ ▁ph ⊔ ư ⊔ ơ ⊔ ng ⊔ ▁ ⊔ đ ⊔ ư ⊔ a ⊔ ▁tin ⊔ ▁m ⊔ ộ ⊔ t ⊔ ▁ph ⊔ ư ⊔ ơ ⊔ ng ⊔ ▁ti ⊔ ệ ⊔ n ⊔ ▁ch ⊔ ữ ⊔ a ⊔ ▁ch ⊔ á ⊔ y ⊔ ▁s ⊔ ân ⊔ ▁bay ⊔ ▁ ⊔ đ ⊔ ã ⊔ ▁t ⊔ ớ ⊔ i ⊔ ▁k ⊔ hi ⊔ ▁tr ⊔ ả ⊔ ▁l ⊔ ờ ⊔ i ⊔ .
250K_S+B	16	▁Local ⊔ ▁media ⊔ ▁report ⊔ s ⊔ ▁an ⊔ ▁air ⊔ port ⊔ ▁fire ⊔ ▁vehicle ⊔ ▁rolle ⊔ d ⊔ ▁over ⊔ ▁while ⊔ ▁respond ⊔ ing ⊔ .	23	▁La ⊔ ▁prensa ⊔ ▁local ⊔ ▁inform ⊔ ó ⊔ ▁que ⊔ ▁una ⊔ ▁patru ⊔ lla ⊔ ▁de ⊔ ▁bombe ⊔ ros ⊔ ▁del ⊔ ▁aero ⊔ pu ⊔ erto ⊔ ▁vol ⊔ có ⊔ ▁mientras ⊔ ▁presta ⊔ ba ⊔ ▁servicio ⊔ .	20	▁Truyền ⊔ ▁thông ⊔ ▁địa ⊔ ▁phương ⊔ ▁đưa ⊔ ▁tin ⊔ ▁một ⊔ ▁phương ⊔ ▁tiện ⊔ ▁chữa ⊔ ▁chá ⊔ y ⊔ ▁sân ⊔ ▁bay ⊔ ▁đã ⊔ ▁tới ⊔ ▁khi ⊔ ▁trả ⊔ ▁lời ⊔ .
64K_S+B	19	▁Lo ⊔ cal ⊔ ▁media ⊔ ▁report ⊔ s ⊔ ▁an ⊔ ▁air ⊔ port ⊔ ▁fire ⊔ ▁ve ⊔ hi ⊔ cle ⊔ ▁rol ⊔ led ⊔ ▁over ⊔ ▁while ⊔ ▁respond ⊔ ing ⊔ .	30	▁La ⊔ ▁pren ⊔ sa ⊔ ▁local ⊔ ▁inform ⊔ ó ⊔ ▁que ⊔ ▁una ⊔ ▁pat ⊔ ru ⊔ lla ⊔ ▁de ⊔ ▁bo ⊔ mber ⊔ os ⊔ ▁del ⊔ ▁a ⊔ ero ⊔ pu ⊔ erto ⊔ ▁vol ⊔ c ⊔ ó ⊔ ▁ ⊔ mien ⊔ tras ⊔ ▁presta ⊔ ba ⊔ ▁servicio ⊔ .	27	▁Tr ⊔ uyền ⊔ ▁thông ⊔ ▁địa ⊔ ▁phương ⊔ ▁đưa ⊔ ▁tin ⊔ ▁một ⊔ ▁phương ⊔ ▁t ⊔ iện ⊔ ▁ch ⊔ ữ ⊔ a ⊔ ▁ ⊔ chá ⊔ y ⊔ ▁s ⊔ ân ⊔ ▁bay ⊔ ▁đã ⊔ ▁tới ⊔ ▁khi ⊔ ▁trả ⊔ ▁l ⊔ ời ⊔ .

Table 8: Tokenization examples obtained from the dev set in Flores+ (1/3). The '⊔' and '▁' symbols indicate the token delimiter and space character of SentencePiece, respectively.

Tokenizer/ vocabulary	Japanese #Tokens	Japanese Sample	Chinese #Tokens	Chinese Sample	Arabic #Tokens	Arabic Sample
M2M-100	27	▁⊔地⊔元⊔メ⊔ディ⊔ア⊔の⊔報⊔道⊔によ⊔ると⊔、⊔空⊔港⊔の⊔消⊔防⊔車⊔が⊔対応⊔中に⊔横⊔転⊔した⊔ということ⊔です⊔。	21	▁当⊔地⊔媒体⊔报道⊔，⊔一⊔辆⊔机场⊔消⊔防⊔车⊔在⊔响⊔应⊔火⊔警⊔时⊔翻⊔了⊔车⊔。	24	▁⊔الإعلام▁⊔وسائل▁⊔أ⊔علنت▁ ⊔ل⊔□قلاب▁⊔عن▁⊔□مح⊔□ية الإ⊔طف⊔اء▁⊔سي⊔ارا□▁⊔حدى ⊔لا⊔طف▁⊔توجه⊔ها▁⊔أثناء▁⊔ ⊔□ح⊔ريق▁⊔اء.
mBART/XLM-R	20	▁⊔地⊔元⊔メディア⊔の⊔報道⊔によると⊔、⊔空港⊔の⊔消防⊔車⊔が⊔対応⊔中⊔に⊔横⊔転⊔した⊔ということです⊔。	17	▁⊔当地⊔媒体报道⊔，⊔一辆⊔机场⊔消防⊔车⊔在⊔响应⊔火⊔警⊔时⊔翻⊔了⊔车⊔。	20	□محلية▁⊔الإعلام▁⊔وسائل▁⊔أعلنت▁ سيارا□▁⊔إحدى▁⊔□قلاب▁⊔عن▁⊔ ⊔توجه▁⊔أثناء▁⊔الإ⊔طف⊔اء▁⊔ ⊔□حر⊔يق▁⊔لإ⊔طف⊔اء▁⊔ها.
NLLB-200	18	▁地⊔元⊔メディア⊔の⊔報道⊔によると⊔、⊔空港⊔の⊔消防⊔車が⊔対応⊔中に⊔横⊔転⊔した⊔ということです⊔。	22	▁当⊔地⊔媒体⊔报⊔道⊔，▁⊔一⊔辆⊔机⊔场⊔消防⊔车⊔在⊔响⊔应⊔火⊔警⊔时⊔翻⊔了⊔车⊔。	30	⊔الإ▁⊔وس⊔ائل▁⊔أ⊔عل⊔□ت▁ □قلاب▁⊔عن▁⊔□مح⊔□ية▁⊔ع⊔لام ⊔الإ▁⊔سي⊔ارا□▁⊔إح⊔دى▁⊔ تو⊔جهه⊔ا▁⊔أث⊔□اء▁⊔طف⊔اء ⊔□ح⊔ريق▁⊔لإ⊔طف⊔اء▁⊔.
mT5	18	▁⊔地元⊔メディア⊔の⊔報道⊔によると⊔、⊔空港⊔の⊔消防⊔車が⊔対応⊔中に⊔横⊔転⊔した⊔ということです⊔。	18	▁⊔当地⊔媒体⊔报道⊔，⊔一辆⊔机场⊔消防⊔车⊔在⊔响应⊔火⊔警⊔时⊔翻⊔了⊔车⊔。	31	ال⊔إعلام▁⊔و⊔سائل▁⊔أع⊔□نت▁ ▁⊔□قلاب⊔▁⊔عن▁⊔□مح⊔□ية▁⊔ الإ⊔طف▁⊔سيارا□⊔▁⊔إح⊔دى⊔ توجه⊔ها⊔▁⊔أث⊔□اء⊔▁⊔اء⊔ ⊔□حر⊔يق▁⊔لإ⊔طف⊔اء▁⊔.
LlaMa2	48	▁⊔地⊔元⊔メ⊔デ⊔ィ⊔ア⊔の⊔報⊔道⊔に⊔よ⊔る⊔と⊔、⊔空⊔港⊔の⊔消⊔<0xE9>⊔<0x98>⊔<0xB2>⊔車⊔が⊔<0xE5>⊔<0xAF>⊔<0xBE>⊔<0xE5>⊔<0xBF>⊔<0x9C>⊔中⊔に⊔<0xE6>⊔<0xA8>⊔<0xAA>⊔<0xE8>⊔<0xBB>⊔<0xA2>⊔し⊔た⊔と⊔い⊔う⊔こ⊔と⊔で⊔す⊔。	43	▁⊔当⊔地⊔<0xE5>⊔<0xAA>⊔<0x92>⊔体⊔<0xE6>⊔<0x8A>⊔<0xA5>⊔道⊔，⊔一⊔<0xE8>⊔<0xBE>⊔<0x86>⊔机⊔场⊔消⊔<0xE9>⊔<0x98>⊔<0xB2>⊔<0xE8>⊔<0xBD>⊔<0xA6>⊔在⊔<0xE5>⊔<0x93>⊔<0x8D>⊔应⊔火⊔<0xE8>⊔<0xAD>⊔<0xA6>⊔时⊔<0xE7>⊔<0xBF>⊔<0xBB>⊔了⊔<0xE8>⊔<0xBD>⊔<0xA6>⊔。	78	و⊔س▁⊔أ⊔ع⊔ل⊔□⊔□⊔▁ ⊔ال⊔إ⊔ع⊔ل⊔ا▁⊔ا⊔ئ⊔ل⊔ ع▁⊔ال⊔م⊔ح⊔ل⊔ي⊔ة▁⊔م ⊔ا⊔□⊔ق⊔ل⊔ا⊔ب▁⊔□⊔ س⊔ي⊔ا▁⊔إ⊔ح⊔د⊔ى⊔▁ ⊔ال⊔إ⊔ط⊔ف⊔ا▁⊔ر⊔ا⊔□⊔ □⊔▁⊔أ⊔ث⊔□⊔ا⊔ء▁⊔ء ل⊔إ⊔ط▁⊔و⊔ج⊔ه⊔ا⊔ ال⊔ح⊔ر⊔ي⊔ق▁⊔ف⊔ا⊔ء⊔ ⊔.
250K_S+B	20	▁⊔地⊔元⊔メディア⊔の⊔報道⊔によると⊔、⊔空港⊔の⊔消防⊔車⊔が⊔対応⊔中⊔に⊔横⊔転⊔した⊔ということです⊔。	17	▁⊔当地⊔媒体报道⊔，⊔一辆⊔机场⊔消防⊔车⊔在⊔响应⊔火⊔警⊔时⊔翻⊔了⊔车⊔。	20	□محلية▁⊔الإعلام▁⊔وسائل▁⊔أعلنت▁ سيارا□▁⊔إحدى▁⊔□قلاب▁⊔عن▁⊔ ⊔توجه▁⊔أثناء▁⊔الإ⊔طف⊔اء▁⊔ ⊔□حر⊔يق▁⊔لإ⊔طف⊔اء▁⊔ها.
64K_S+B	28	▁⊔地⊔元⊔メ⊔ディ⊔ア⊔の⊔報⊔道⊔による⊔と⊔、⊔空⊔港⊔の⊔消⊔防⊔車⊔が⊔対応⊔中⊔に⊔横⊔転⊔した⊔ということ⊔です⊔。	21	▁⊔当地⊔媒体⊔报道⊔，⊔一⊔辆⊔机场⊔消⊔防⊔车⊔在⊔响⊔应⊔火⊔警⊔时⊔翻⊔了⊔车⊔。	30	⊔ال▁⊔و⊔سائل▁⊔أع⊔ل⊔□ت▁ ▁⊔عن▁⊔□مح⊔ل⊔ية▁⊔إعلام س⊔يارا□▁⊔إ⊔ح⊔دى▁⊔□قلاب توجه▁⊔أ⊔ثناء▁⊔الإ⊔طف⊔اء▁⊔ ⊔□حر⊔يق▁⊔لإ⊔طف⊔اء▁⊔ها⊔ .

Table 9: Tokenization examples obtained from the dev set in Flores+ (2/3). The '⊔' and '▁' symbols indicate the token delimiter and space character of SentencePiece, respectively.

Tokenizer/ vocabulary	Hindi #Tokens	Hindi Sample	Russian #Tokens	Russian Sample
M2M-100	28	▁स्थानीय␣▁मीडिया␣▁ने␣▁ बताया␣▁है␣▁कि␣▁कार␣्र␣ वाई␣▁करने␣▁के␣▁दौरान␣▁ एयर␣पोर्ट␣▁का␣▁अ␣ग्␣नि ␣शा␣मक␣▁वा␣हन␣▁लु␣ढ़ ␣क␣▁गया␣▁□ा␣.	26	▁Ме␣ст␣ные␣▁СМИ␣▁соо б␣ща␣ют␣,␣▁что␣▁в␣▁а э␣ропо␣рту␣▁по␣▁пути␣ ▁на␣▁вы␣зов␣▁пере␣вер␣ ну␣лась␣▁пожар␣ная␣▁ма шина␣.
mBART/XLM-R	22	▁स्थानीय␣▁मीडिया␣▁ने␣▁ बताया␣▁है␣▁कि␣▁कार्रवाई␣▁ करने␣▁के␣▁दौरान␣▁एयरपोर्ट ␣▁का␣▁अग्नि␣शा␣मक␣▁ वाहन␣▁लु␣ढ़␣क␣▁गया␣▁ □ा␣.	22	▁Мес␣т␣ные␣▁СМИ␣▁со ␣обща␣ют␣,␣▁что␣▁в␣▁ аэропорт␣у␣▁по␣▁пути␣▁ на␣▁вызов␣▁пере␣вернулас ь␣▁пожар␣ная␣▁машина␣.
NLLB-200	23	▁स्थानीय␣▁मीडिया␣▁ने␣▁ बताया␣▁है␣▁कि␣▁कार्रवाई␣▁ करने␣▁के␣▁दौरान␣▁एयर␣ पोर्ट␣▁का␣▁अग्नि␣शा␣मक␣ ▁वाहन␣▁लु␣ढ़␣क␣▁गया␣▁ □ा␣.	27	▁Ме␣ст␣ные␣▁С␣М␣И␣ ▁сооб␣ща␣ют␣,␣▁что␣▁в ␣▁аэро␣порту␣▁по␣▁пути ␣▁на␣▁выз␣ов␣▁пере␣вер ␣ну␣лась␣▁пожар␣ная␣▁м ашина␣.
mT5	36	▁स्थान␣ीय␣▁मी␣डिया␣▁ने␣ ▁बता␣या␣▁है␣▁कि␣▁कार्␣ र␣वाई␣▁कर␣ने␣▁के␣▁द␣ौ ␣रान␣▁ए␣यर␣पोर्ट␣▁का␣ ▁अ␣ग्नि␣शा␣मक␣▁␣वाह␣ न␣▁लु␣ढ़␣क␣▁ग␣या␣▁□ा ␣.	25	▁␣Мест␣ные␣▁С␣МИ␣▁с ообщ␣ают␣,␣▁что␣▁в␣▁а эро␣порту␣▁по␣▁␣пути␣ ▁на␣▁выз␣ов␣▁пере␣верну ␣лась␣▁пожар␣ная␣▁маши на␣.
LlaMa2	102	▁␣स␣्␣□␣ा␣न␣ी␣य ␣▁␣म␣ी␣ड␣ि␣य␣ा␣ ▁␣न␣े␣▁␣ब␣त␣ा␣य␣ ␣▁␣ह␣ै␣▁␣क␣ि␣▁␣ क␣ा␣र␣्␣र␣व␣ा␣ <0xE0>␣<0xA4>␣<0x88>␣▁ ␣क␣र␣न␣े␣▁␣क␣े␣▁ ␣द␣<0xE0>␣<0xA5>␣ <0x8C>␣र␣ा␣न␣▁␣ <0xE0>␣<0xA4>␣<0x8F>␣य ␣र␣प␣ो␣र␣्␣ट␣▁␣क ␣ा␣▁␣अ␣ग␣्␣न␣ि␣ श␣ा␣म␣क␣▁␣व␣ा␣ह ␣न␣▁␣ल␣ु␣<0xE0>␣ <0xA4>␣<0xA2>␣़␣क␣▁ ␣ग␣य␣ा␣▁␣□␣ा␣.	35	▁Ме␣ст␣ные␣▁С␣М␣И␣ ▁сооб␣ща␣ют␣,␣▁что␣▁в ␣▁а␣э␣ро␣пор␣ту␣▁по␣ ▁пу␣ти␣▁на␣▁вы␣зов␣▁п ере␣вер␣ну␣лась␣▁по␣ж ␣ар␣ная␣▁ма␣ши␣на␣.
250K_S+B	22	▁स्थानीय␣▁मीडिया␣▁ने␣▁ बताया␣▁है␣▁कि␣▁कार्रवाई␣▁ करने␣▁के␣▁दौरान␣▁एयरपोर्ट ␣▁का␣▁अग्नि␣शा␣मक␣▁ वाहन␣▁लु␣ढ़␣क␣▁गया␣▁ □ा␣.	23	▁Мес␣т␣ные␣▁СМИ␣▁соо бща␣ют␣,␣▁что␣▁в␣▁аэр опорт␣у␣▁по␣▁пути␣▁на␣ ▁вы␣зов␣▁пере␣верну␣лас ь␣▁пожар␣ная␣▁машина␣.
64K_S+B	29	▁स्थानीय␣▁मीडिया␣▁ने␣▁ बताया␣▁है␣▁कि␣▁कार␣्र␣ वाई␣▁करने␣▁के␣▁दौरान␣▁ए ␣यर␣पोर्ट␣▁का␣▁अ␣ग्नि␣ शा␣मक␣▁वा␣हन␣▁␣लु␣ढ़ ␣क␣▁गया␣▁□ा␣.	30	▁Ме␣ст␣ные␣▁С␣МИ␣▁с ообщ␣а␣ют␣,␣▁что␣▁в␣ ▁а␣эр␣опо␣рту␣▁по␣▁пу т␣и␣▁на␣▁вы␣зов␣▁пере ␣верну␣лась␣▁по␣жар␣на я␣▁машин␣а␣.

Table 10: Tokenization examples obtained from the dev set in Flores+ (3/3). The '␣' and '▁' symbols indicate the token delimiter and space character of SentencePiece, respectively.

Machine Translation Of Marathi Dialects: A Case Study Of Kadodi

Raj Dabre[1,2] **Mary Noel Dabre**[3] **Teresa Pereira**[4]
National Institute of Information and Communications Technology, Kyoto, Japan[1]
IIT Madras, Chennai, India[2]
Independent, Vasai, India[3]
St Gonsalo Garcia College, Vasai, India[4]
raj.dabre@nict.go.jp

Abstract

While Marathi is considered as a low- to middle-resource language, its 42 dialects have mostly been ignored, mainly because these dialects are mostly spoken and rarely written, making them extremely low-resource. In this paper we explore the machine translation (MT) of Kadodi, also known as Samvedi, which is a dialect of Marathi. We first discuss the Kadodi dialect, highlighting the differences from the standard dialect, followed by presenting a manually curated dataset called ***Suman*** consisting of a trilingual Kadodi-Marathi-English dictionary of 949 entries and 942 simple sentence triples and idioms created by native Kadodi speakers. We then evaluate 3 existing large language models (LLMs) supporting Marathi, namely Gemma-2-9b, Sarvam-2b-0.5 and LLaMa-3.1-8b, in few-shot prompting style to determine their efficacy for translation involving Kadodi. We observe that these models exhibit rather lackluster performance in handling Kadodi even for simple sentences, indicating a dire situation.

1 Introduction

Marathi is a language primarily spoken by about 83 million people[1] in the Indian state of Maharashtra. Across the world, while a standard dialect of any language exists, a substantial portion of these speakers also speak a local dialect and Marathi is no exception. There are 42 known dialects of Marathi[2] a vast majority of which, if not all, are spoken rather than written, which makes natural language processing (NLP) for such dialects extremely hard. However, excluding these dialects from NLP systems would lead to a cultural representation imbalance, since a significant amount of culture is connected to languages and their dialects. Given the massive Marathi dialect-speaking population, we consider it important to take steps to include them in NLP systems, the first being via resource creation and evaluation.

In this paper we focus on a minor dialect of Marathi, namely, Kadodi[3], also known as Samvedi, which is spoken in the Vasai[4] region of Maharashtra and has about 60,000 native speakers. The Kadodi language is a mix of Konkani, Gujarati, Marathi and Indo-Portuguese (now extinct). The speakers of Kadodi are known colloquially as Kuparis[5][6] which essentially means comrade and is a term used to call one's child's godfather. The Kupari people are descendants of a mixture of Samvedi Brahmins, Goan Konkani Brahmins and Portuguese New Christians; because of intermarriages between them. Due to it being a spoken dialect, it has been passed down over the generations mainly via conversations. However, this also means that there is no proper text data available for NLP applications.

In this paper, we present the first of its kind study of Kadodi taking Machine Translation (MT) as a NLP application. We first describe the features of the Kadodi language and explain its differences from Marathi. Then, we describe the process of data collection, which was mainly done via two native speakers of Kadodi, leading to ***Suman***, the first tri-parallel Kadodi-Marathi-English dataset. Finally, we attempt to evaluate the translation quality of Kadodi translation both to and from English and Marathi via few-shot prompting of 3 LLMs. where we show that despite our evaluation being conducted on simple sentences, all LLMs we considered exhibit lackluster performance, indicating the need for dedicated pre-training and fine-tuning

[1]https://en.wikipedia.org/wiki/Marathi_language

[2]https://en.wikipedia.org/wiki/Marathi_language#Dialects

[3]https://en.wikipedia.org/wiki/Kadodi_language

[4]https://en.wikipedia.org/wiki/Vasai

[5]https://en.wikipedia.org/wiki/Kupari

[6]The feminine form of Kupari is Kumari.

Proceedings of the Eleventh Workshop on Asian Translation (WAT 2024), pages 36–44
November 16, 2024

on dialectic data. Our contributions are as follows:

1. The first study of Kadodi machine translation.

2. A novel dataset called ***Suman***, for Kadodi-Marathi-English 3-way parallel entries with about 1,900 dictionary and sentence pairs, totally. We release our dataset publicly[7].

3. An evaluation of the translation quality of existing models involving Kadodi.

Going forward, Kadodi refers to the Kadodi dialect and Marathi refers to the standard dialect.

2 Related Work

This paper mainly focuses on the natural language processing of dialects, specifically machine translation involving the Kadodi dialect of Marathi.

A vast majority of the dialectic work has been conducted on Arabic, English and French dialects, and some of the most prominent works have been on dialect understanding (Baimukan et al., 2022; Zampieri et al., 2014; Malmasi et al., 2016; Goutte et al., 2016; Elmadany et al., 2018; Joukhadar et al., 2019) and dialect translation (Zbib et al., 2012; Bouamor et al., 2018; Contarino, 2021; Lent et al., 2024; Robinson et al., 2024)[8]. On the other hand, works on summarization (Olabisi et al., 2022; Keswani and Celis, 2021) and dialogue (Elmadany et al., 2018; Joukhadar et al., 2019; Marietto et al., 2013) are rather limited due to the unavailability of data or lack of permissive licenses.

Since dialects are closely related to their standard variant, multilingual transfer learning (Dabre et al., 2020) approaches are often helpful alongside approaches leveraging transliteration (J et al., 2024; Dabre et al., 2022). Additionally, character level systems (Abe et al., 2018) are often effective in settings where the training data for dialects is rather limited, where regularization approaches are also effective (Liu et al., 2022; Maurya et al., 2023). In low-resource settings, it becomes important to leverage linguistic features, ideally of dialects, to improve translation quality (Erdmann et al., 2017; Chakrabarty et al., 2022, 2020). On the other hand, since many dialects are spoken, some researcher focus directly on creating and leveraging speech data (Plüss et al., 2023). Joshi et al. (2024) give a comprehensive survey of NLP for dialects across the world, and we encourage readers to read it for an in-depth understanding of the prominent works carried out in this area.

Works on dialects of Indian languages are rather nonexistent, with a few exceptions (Maurya et al., 2023). To the best of our knowledge, this is the first work on machine translation involving Kadodi and in general on any dialect of Marathi.

[7]https://github.com/prajdabre/kadodinlp

[8]To be accurate, Lent et al. (2024) and Robinson et al. (2024) focus on Creoles and not dialects. However, we list these works as applicable to dialects because of the high similarity between Creoles and their ancestor languages, which is analogous to the similarity between dialects.

Kadodi	Marathi	English
लात (lat)	लाथ (lath)	kick
दुद (dud)	दूध (dudh)	milk
ऑजा (auja)	ओझे (ooje)	burden
शार (shaar)	चार (char)	four
हॅन (haen)	शेण (shen)	cowdung
हन (hun)	सण (sun)	festival

Table 1: Representative Kadodi words with their Marathi and English equivalents and pronunciations.

3 *Suman*: A Kadodi Parallel Corpus

We first give details about the Kadodi dialect contrasting it with Marathi followed by a description of the Kadodi parallel corpus we created from scratch, which we refer to as ***Suman***. This consists of a trilingual Kadodi-Marathi-English dictionary and simple, short sentences.

3.1 Kadodi Language

Given that Kadodi is a dialect of Marathi, it exhibits an extremely high degree of similarity with the latter, with very few lexical and grammatical differences. We now briefly explain some key differences as follows:

Vowels and Consonants: Marathi primarily uses 14 vowels[9] and 34 consonants. However, since Kadodi is primarily a spoken language, it does not use 2 out of 14 vowels, namely, ऐ (ay) and औ (au), and 4 out of 34 consonants, namely, च (cha), छ (ccha), ण (na), and ष (sha). The reasons for this is unknown and undocumented due to the spoken nature of Kadodi, but consonant dropping[10] is a common feature in dialects.

[9]Since not everyone is familiar with IPA, we refer readers to take a look here for an easier reference on how to better read these characters.

[10]https://en.wikipedia.org/wiki/Phonological_history_of_English_consonant_clusters

Language	Sentence
Kadodi	तॉ मजुरी करॉन पॉट भरतॅ tou majuri karon pout bhartae
Marathi	तो मजुरी करून पोट भरतो to majuri karun pot bharto
English	He makes a living by working as a laborer
Kadodi	तॉ निजलॅ tou nejlay
Marathi	तो झोपला आहे to zhopla ahe
English	He is sleeping

Table 2: Examples of Kadodi sentences along with their Marathi and English translations and transliterations.

Kadodi Vocabulary: Table 1 gives a list of some words in Kadodi with their pronunciations, alongside Marathi and English translations. The reader will be able to note that the words look mostly similar, and the key differences lies in the consonant usage. For example, the word for cow dung is हॅन (haen) [Marathi word is शेण (shen)], where the key difference is the use of हॅ (hae) in place of शे (she). Note that it is fairly common for श (sha) and स (sa) to be replaced with ह (ha) in Kadodi. Kadodi also differs from Marathi in that it prefers to use voiced or voiceless dental plosives [त (ta) द (da)] instead of aspirated and murmured ones [थ (tha) ध (dha)]. Note that a stark change in consonants does not occur, and often the changes are rather minor. For example, a plan nasal labial consonant will never be replaced by a fricative glottal one.

Kadodi Grammar: In Table 2 we give examples of Kadodi sentences to highlight the subtle differences with Marathi. As can be seen, the Marathi and Kadodi sentences sound mostly similar. The main difference is in the word forms भरतॅ (bharte) vs भरतो (bharto), and the word choices, निजलॅ (nijley) vs झोपला[11] (zhopla). Another interesting difference is that in Marathi we use झोपला आहे (zhopla ahe) to say "(he/she) is sleeping" (present tense) where आहे (ahe) is the verb for "is" or "to be", however, in Kadodi, although आहे (ahe) can be translated as हाय (hai), it is often omitted for the present tense.

Although there are other minor differences between Marathi and Kadodi, we refer the readers to Russell and Cohn (2012); Francis Correia (1992) for detailed overviews. We also point to a book on the Kadodi (Samvedi) community by Pereira (2007). There are also magazines[12] in Kadodi for interested readers.

[11] झोपणे (zhopne) is the more commonly used word for sleeping, whereas निजणे (nizne) is less commonly used in Marathi.

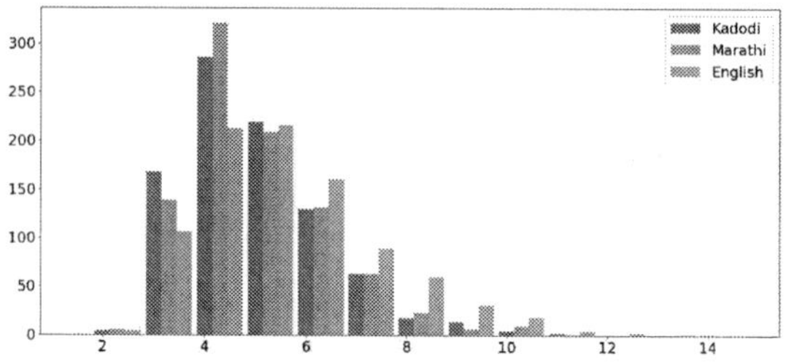

Figure 1: Distribution of Kadodi, Marathi and English sentence lengths.

3.2 Data Collection

We now describe how we collected data for Kadodi MT to create ***Suman***. We primarily focused on collecting Kadodi-Marathi data, since the native speakers (annotators) of both dialects do not possess native English proficiency. The annotators were asked to freely construct any sentences which came to mind, as long as they considered them to be useful in daily conversations. Therefore, the domain of the dataset can be said to be a mix of general domain, conversational and daily use. As much as possible, we asked the annotators to provide English translations, which were manually corrected by native speakers. Annotators were asked to provide dictionary entries as well simple phrases/sentences, leaving longer, complex sentences for the future. All the data was collected over the span of 1 month via Google sheets. We had 2 annotators, and they provided a total of 949 tri-parallel dictionary entries and 942 tri-parallel short sentences. Due to lack of funds, both annotators agreed to create data for free, and for compensation, they were given authorship of this paper.

Dictionary: With the help of annotators, we have procured a dictionary of 949 entries, starting with all 30 consonants and 12 vowels used in Kadodi. Furthermore, the annotators have ensured that for each consonant and vowel type, there are at least 4 Kadodi words. This dictionary also contains roughly 200 instances of numbers, common foods, animals and birds, days of the week, names of months, family relationships, daily use words,

[12] `https://kadodi.in/`

Shots	kad-mar			kad-eng			mar-kad			eng-kad		
	S	G	L	S	G	L	S	G	L	S	G	L
1	17.0	30.3	37.0	24.3	25.7	28.7	20.2	28.5	30.1	13.2	15.7	18.6
4	22.8	35.4	42.0	24.9	31.4	32.2	18.3	30.4	**33.5**	14.3	15.3	19.4
8	24.4	35.9	42.1	24.3	31.3	32.0	20.0	30.2	32.3	17.1	13.0	**19.6**
12	24.3	36.6	**42.8**	23.1	**33.1**	32.6	18.5	30.2	32.3	16.5	14.2	18.7

Table 3: chrF scores of translation for Kadodi-Marathi (kad-mar), Kadodi-English (kad-eng), Marathi-Kadodi (mar-kad) and English-Kadodi (eng-kad) with 1, 4, 8 and 12 shots. We have compared Sarvam-2b-0.5 (S), Gemma-2-9b (G) and LLaMa-3.1-8b (L) models.

parts of the body, seasons and comparative words.
Sentences: In addition to the dictionaries, the annotators also created 912 Kadodi sentences of 2199 unique words along with their Marathi and English translations of 1924 and 1650 unique words, respectively. The sentence length distribution is shown in Figure 1. As is evident, most of these are short phrases and sentences between 2 and 6 words, and the length distributions are mostly similar. Note that, Kadodi and Marathi are both morphologically rich languages, so a word can often be the equivalent of a sentence via agglutination. Therefore, just because the sentence lengths appear to be short, they are not all necessarily short in the content they encapsulate. The annotators also created 30 Kadodi idioms along with their literal Marathi translations and explanations in Marathi and English, leading to 942 triples. However, we do not consider these for our experiments.

4 Experiments

We now describe some simple experiments we conduct for Kadodi⇔English and Kadodi⇔Marathi translation using LLMs.

4.1 Settings

For our experiments, we only focus on the parallel sentences part of ***Suman***. Of the 942 Kadodi-Marathi-English triples, we randomly choose 12 triples for 1, 4, 8 and 12-shot prompting and set them aside. Note, once again, we also set aside 30 idiom triples. This leaves us with 900 triples for testing. As for the models, we use Sarvam-2b-v0.5[13] a 2 billion parameter model, Gemma-2-9b (Team et al., 2024) a 9 billion parameter model, and LLaMA-3.1-8b (Dubey et al., 2024) an 8 billion parameter model. All 3 models have seen Indian languages during pre-training although, Sarvam-2b-0.5 has been trained exclusively for English and Indian languages, including Marathi, on a total of 1 trillion tokens each. A brief evaluation[14] of these models on Konkani, Gujarati and Marathi MT reveals that they have reasonable translation capabilities via few-shot prompting. We perform greedy decoding without sampling up to 64 new tokens and use chrF for evaluation.

4.2 Results

Table 3 gives the chrF scores[15] for Kadodi-Marathi, Kadodi-English, Marathi-Kadodi and English-Kadodi translation with varying number of shots.

1. Generating Kadodi is challenging: As can be seen, translation into English and Marathi yields better chrF scores than into Kadodi. We found that since the models were not trained on Kadodi, translating into Kadodi leads to very poor translations. In fact, a manual evaluation showed that most of the time the generated translations were in Marathi with some Kadodi word forms. Pronouns and standalone verbs like (is, am, are) are often well handled. In a number of cases for the Sarvam-2b-0.5 model, the Kadodi translations have nothing to do with the sentence being translated, when the source language is English. This is a form of off-target hallucinations. However, Gemma-2-9b and LLaMa-3.1-8b are vastly better. Also note that these models have an easier time handling translation between Marathi and Kadodi compared to translation between English and Kadodi. This is likely because the models have less overhead translating between dialects.

2. Limited impact of shots: Although LLMs are

[13]`https://huggingface.co/sarvamai/sarvam-2b-v0.5`

[14]Since we do not possess any resources for Indo-Portuguese evaluation we skip this but given that Indo-Portuguese is a variation of Portuguese, we expect LLaMa and Gemma to do far better than Sarvam.

[15]nrefs:1 | case:mixed | eff:yes | nc:6 | nw:0 | space:no | version:2.4.1

touted to work well in few-shot settings, even for languages not seen before, we expected that increasing the number of shots would condition the model to better handle Kadodi. For the Sarvam-2b-0.5 model, this is highly translation direction dependent, where Kadodi-Marathi and English-Kadodi generation benefits from increasing shots, but the other two directions barely benefit from shots. On the other hand, LLaMa-3.1-8b and Gemma-2-9b do a significantly better job. Increasing shots from 1 to 4 leads to a large performance jump, but beyond this the gains are minor for up to 12 shots. Comparing Sarvam, Gemma and LLaMa models, it appears that scale indeed is important. Although the latter two models are not intentionally designed for Marathi, they do better and the key difference is the size of the models. Furthermore, the Sarvam model is trained on a vast amount of synthetic data, which might be detrimental.

Since none of the models does particularly well for generating Kadodi, despite our evaluation sentences being simple, we suspect that the reason for this is that they have not seen a shred of Kadodi and even though, it is a dialect of Marathi. They likely consider Kadodi as a garbled version of Marathi. Following the principle of GIGO[16], since the inputs and expected outputs are what the models perceive as noise, the generated content is fairly noisy. This indicates the need for incorporating monolingual Kadodi knowledge into these models, something we leave for future work.

5 Conclusion

In this paper, we presented the first of its kind study of machine translation of Kadodi, a dialect of Marathi spoken in the Vasai region of Maharashtra, India. We described the features of Kadodi and, ***Suman***, a Kadodi-Marathi-English dataset, which was manually created, spanning close to 1,900 tri-parallel entries. Our automatic evaluation showed that Kadodi translation via few-shot prompting of LLMs, even on an Indic exclusive pre-trained language model which as been trained for 1 trillion Indic tokens including Marathi, is still rather poor. This shows that existing LMs, do not handle Kadodi, and likely other dialects of Marathi, indicating a dire situation. However, this means that the field of NLP of Marathi dialects is ripe for exploration. In the future, we would like to expand our dataset, not only to include additional parallel sentences but also branch out to other tasks like summarization, headline generation and question answering, to name a few.

[16] `https://en.wikipedia.org/wiki/Garbage_in,_garbage_out`

Limitations

This paper focuses on a rather simple case of Kadodi translation, where the resources are small dictionaries and short sentences. However, we plan to scale up data collection and cover more complex sentences spanning multiple domains, subject to annotator availability and budget. We also do not focus on fine-tuning LLMs due to the non-availability of training corpora, but we expect this to be sorted out as our data collection efforts ramp up.

Acknowledgements

Raj Dabre would first like to thank his mother, Mary, who is also the second author, for being an outstanding mother. She carried him as a kid and now hard carries this whole Kadodi NLP project as an annotator and language expert. At the same time, he thanks his honorable father, Noel, and his loving family in general. He also thanks Teresa, the third author, for her enthusiasm and support, along with the entire Kadodi community, which is extremely proud of its language and heritage. Finally, an ode to a great Kadodi person: कहिक्का (kahikka).

References

Kaori Abe, Yuichiroh Matsubayashi, Naoaki Okazaki, and Kentaro Inui. 2018. Multi-dialect neural machine translation and dialectometry. In *Proceedings of the 32nd Pacific Asia Conference on Language, Information and Computation*, Hong Kong. Association for Computational Linguistics.

Nurpeiis Baimukan, Houda Bouamor, and Nizar Habash. 2022. Hierarchical aggregation of dialectal data for arabic dialect identification. In *Proceedings of the Thirteenth Language Resources and Evaluation Conference*, pages 4586–4596.

Houda Bouamor, Nizar Habash, Mohammad Salameh, Wajdi Zaghouani, Owen Rambow, Dana Abdulrahim, Ossama Obeid, Salam Khalifa, Fadhl Eryani, Alexander Erdmann, and Kemal Oflazer. 2018. The MADAR Arabic dialect corpus and lexicon. In *Proceedings of the Eleventh International Conference on Language Resources and Evaluation (LREC 2018)*, Miyazaki, Japan. European Language Resources Association (ELRA).

Abhisek Chakrabarty, Raj Dabre, Chenchen Ding, Hideki Tanaka, Masao Utiyama, and Eiichiro Sumita. 2022. FeatureBART: Feature based sequence-to-sequence pre-training for low-resource NMT. In *Proceedings of the 29th International Conference on Computational Linguistics*, pages 5014–5020, Gyeongju, Republic of Korea. International Committee on Computational Linguistics.

Abhisek Chakrabarty, Raj Dabre, Chenchen Ding, Masao Utiyama, and Eiichiro Sumita. 2020. Improving low-resource NMT through relevance based linguistic features incorporation. In *Proceedings of the 28th International Conference on Computational Linguistics*, pages 4263–4274, Barcelona, Spain (Online). International Committee on Computational Linguistics.

Antonio Contarino. 2021. Neural machine translation adaptation and automatic terminology evaluation: a case study on italian and south tyrolean german legal texts.

Raj Dabre, Chenhui Chu, and Anoop Kunchukuttan. 2020. A survey of multilingual neural machine translation. *ACM Comput. Surv.*, 53(5).

Raj Dabre, Himani Shrotriya, Anoop Kunchukuttan, Ratish Puduppully, Mitesh Khapra, and Pratyush Kumar. 2022. IndicBART: A pre-trained model for indic natural language generation. In *Findings of the Association for Computational Linguistics: ACL 2022*, pages 1849–1863, Dublin, Ireland. Association for Computational Linguistics.

Abhimanyu Dubey, Abhinav Jauhri, Abhinav Pandey, Abhishek Kadian, Ahmad Al-Dahle, Aiesha Letman, Akhil Mathur, Alan Schelten, Amy Yang, Angela Fan, Anirudh Goyal, Anthony Hartshorn, Aobo Yang, Archi Mitra, Archie Sravankumar, Artem Korenev, Arthur Hinsvark, Arun Rao, Aston Zhang, Aurelien Rodriguez, Austen Gregerson, Ava Spataru, Baptiste Roziere, Bethany Biron, Binh Tang, Bobbie Chern, Charlotte Caucheteux, Chaya Nayak, Chloe Bi, Chris Marra, Chris McConnell, Christian Keller, Christophe Touret, Chunyang Wu, Corinne Wong, Cristian Canton Ferrer, Cyrus Nikolaidis, Damien Allonsius, Daniel Song, Danielle Pintz, Danny Livshits, David Esiobu, Dhruv Choudhary, Dhruv Mahajan, Diego Garcia-Olano, Diego Perino, Dieuwke Hupkes, Egor Lakomkin, Ehab AlBadawy, Elina Lobanova, Emily Dinan, Eric Michael Smith, Filip Radenovic, Frank Zhang, Gabriel Synnaeve, Gabrielle Lee, Georgia Lewis Anderson, Graeme Nail, Gregoire Mialon, Guan Pang, Guillem Cucurell, Hailey Nguyen, Hannah Korevaar, Hu Xu, Hugo Touvron, Iliyan Zarov, Imanol Arrieta Ibarra, Isabel Kloumann, Ishan Misra, Ivan Evtimov, Jade Copet, Jaewon Lee, Jan Geffert, Jana Vranes, Jason Park, Jay Mahadeokar, Jeet Shah, Jelmer van der Linde, Jennifer Billock, Jenny Hong, Jenya Lee, Jeremy Fu, Jianfeng Chi, Jianyu Huang, Jiawen Liu, Jie Wang, Jiecao Yu, Joanna Bitton, Joe Spisak, Jongsoo Park, Joseph Rocca, Joshua Johnstun, Joshua Saxe, Junteng Jia, Kalyan Vasuden Alwala, Kartikeya Upasani, Kate Plawiak, Ke Li, Kenneth Heafield, Kevin Stone, Khalid El-Arini, Krithika Iyer, Kshitiz Malik, Kuenley Chiu, Kunal Bhalla, Lauren Rantala-Yeary, Laurens van der Maaten, Lawrence Chen, Liang Tan, Liz Jenkins, Louis Martin, Lovish Madaan, Lubo Malo, Lukas Blecher, Lukas Landzaat, Luke de Oliveira, Madeline Muzzi, Mahesh Pasupuleti, Mannat Singh, Manohar Paluri, Marcin Kardas, Mathew Oldham, Mathieu Rita, Maya Pavlova, Melanie Kambadur, Mike Lewis, Min Si, Mitesh Kumar Singh, Mona Hassan, Naman Goyal, Narjes Torabi, Nikolay Bashlykov, Nikolay Bogoychev, Niladri Chatterji, Olivier Duchenne, Onur Çelebi, Patrick Alrassy, Pengchuan Zhang, Pengwei Li, Petar Vasic, Peter Weng, Prajjwal Bhargava, Pratik Dubal, Praveen Krishnan, Punit Singh Koura, Puxin Xu, Qing He, Qingxiao Dong, Ragavan Srinivasan, Raj Ganapathy, Ramon Calderer, Ricardo Silveira Cabral, Robert Stojnic, Roberta Raileanu, Rohit Girdhar, Rohit Patel, Romain Sauvestre, Ronnie Polidoro, Roshan Sumbaly, Ross Taylor, Ruan Silva, Rui Hou, Rui Wang, Saghar Hosseini, Sahana Chennabasappa, Sanjay Singh, Sean Bell, Seohyun Sonia Kim, Sergey Edunov, Shaoliang Nie, Sharan Narang, Sharath Raparthy, Sheng Shen, Shengye Wan, Shruti Bhosale, Shun Zhang, Simon Vandenhende, Soumya Batra, Spencer Whitman, Sten Sootla, Stephane Collot, Suchin Gururangan, Sydney Borodinsky, Tamar Herman, Tara Fowler, Tarek Sheasha, Thomas Georgiou, Thomas Scialom, Tobias Speckbacher, Todor Mihaylov, Tong Xiao, Ujjwal Karn, Vedanuj Goswami, Vibhor Gupta, Vignesh Ramanathan, Viktor Kerkez, Vincent Gonguet, Virginie Do, Vish Vogeti, Vladan Petrovic, Weiwei Chu, Wenhan Xiong, Wenyin Fu, Whitney Meers, Xavier Martinet, Xiaodong Wang, Xiaoqing Ellen Tan, Xinfeng Xie, Xuchao Jia, Xuewei Wang, Yaelle Goldschlag, Yashesh Gaur, Yasmine Babaei, Yi Wen, Yiwen Song, Yuchen Zhang, Yue Li, Yuning Mao, Zacharie Delpierre Coudert, Zheng Yan, Zhengxing Chen, Zoe Papakipos, Aaditya Singh, Aaron Grattafiori, Abha Jain, Adam Kelsey, Adam Shajnfeld, Adithya Gangidi, Adolfo Victoria, Ahuva Goldstand, Ajay Menon, Ajay Sharma, Alex Boesenberg, Alex Vaughan, Alexei Baevski, Allie Feinstein, Amanda Kallet, Amit Sangani, Anam Yunus, Andrei Lupu, Andres Alvarado, Andrew Caples, Andrew Gu, Andrew Ho, Andrew Poulton, Andrew Ryan, Ankit Ramchandani, Annie Franco, Aparajita Saraf, Arkabandhu Chowdhury, Ashley Gabriel, Ashwin Bharambe, Assaf Eisenman, Azadeh Yazdan, Beau James, Ben Maurer, Benjamin Leonhardi, Bernie Huang, Beth Loyd, Beto De Paola, Bhargavi Paranjape, Bing Liu, Bo Wu, Boyu Ni, Braden Hancock, Bram Wasti, Brandon Spence, Brani Stojkovic, Brian Gamido, Britt Montalvo, Carl Parker, Carly Burton, Catalina Mejia, Changhan Wang, Changkyu Kim, Chao Zhou, Chester Hu, Ching-Hsiang Chu, Chris Cai, Chris Tindal, Christoph Feichtenhofer, Damon Civin, Dana Beaty, Daniel Kreymer, Daniel Li, Danny Wyatt, David Adkins, David Xu, Davide Testuggine, Delia David, Devi Parikh, Diana Liskovich, Didem Foss, Dingkang

Wang, Duc Le, Dustin Holland, Edward Dowling, Eissa Jamil, Elaine Montgomery, Eleonora Presani, Emily Hahn, Emily Wood, Erik Brinkman, Esteban Arcaute, Evan Dunbar, Evan Smothers, Fei Sun, Felix Kreuk, Feng Tian, Firat Ozgenel, Francesco Caggioni, Francisco Guzmán, Frank Kanayet, Frank Seide, Gabriela Medina Florez, Gabriella Schwarz, Gada Badeer, Georgia Swee, Gil Halpern, Govind Thattai, Grant Herman, Grigory Sizov, Guangyi, Zhang, Guna Lakshminarayanan, Hamid Shojanazeri, Han Zou, Hannah Wang, Hanwen Zha, Haroun Habeeb, Harrison Rudolph, Helen Suk, Henry Aspegren, Hunter Goldman, Ibrahim Damlaj, Igor Molybog, Igor Tufanov, Irina-Elena Veliche, Itai Gat, Jake Weissman, James Geboski, James Kohli, Japhet Asher, Jean-Baptiste Gaya, Jeff Marcus, Jeff Tang, Jennifer Chan, Jenny Zhen, Jeremy Reizenstein, Jeremy Teboul, Jessica Zhong, Jian Jin, Jingyi Yang, Joe Cummings, Jon Carvill, Jon Shepard, Jonathan McPhie, Jonathan Torres, Josh Ginsburg, Junjie Wang, Kai Wu, Kam Hou U, Karan Saxena, Karthik Prasad, Kartikay Khandelwal, Katayoun Zand, Kathy Matosich, Kaushik Veeraraghavan, Kelly Michelena, Keqian Li, Kun Huang, Kunal Chawla, Kushal Lakhotia, Kyle Huang, Lailin Chen, Lakshya Garg, Lavender A, Leandro Silva, Lee Bell, Lei Zhang, Liangpeng Guo, Licheng Yu, Liron Moshkovich, Luca Wehrstedt, Madian Khabsa, Manav Avalani, Manish Bhatt, Maria Tsimpoukelli, Martynas Mankus, Matan Hasson, Matthew Lennie, Matthias Reso, Maxim Groshev, Maxim Naumov, Maya Lathi, Meghan Keneally, Michael L. Seltzer, Michal Valko, Michelle Restrepo, Mihir Patel, Mik Vyatskov, Mikayel Samvelyan, Mike Clark, Mike Macey, Mike Wang, Miquel Jubert Hermoso, Mo Metanat, Mohammad Rastegari, Munish Bansal, Nandhini Santhanam, Natascha Parks, Natasha White, Navyata Bawa, Nayan Singhal, Nick Egebo, Nicolas Usunier, Nikolay Pavlovich Laptev, Ning Dong, Ning Zhang, Norman Cheng, Oleg Chernoguz, Olivia Hart, Omkar Salpekar, Ozlem Kalinli, Parkin Kent, Parth Parekh, Paul Saab, Pavan Balaji, Pedro Rittner, Philip Bontrager, Pierre Roux, Piotr Dollar, Polina Zvyagina, Prashant Ratanchandani, Pritish Yuvraj, Qian Liang, Rachad Alao, Rachel Rodriguez, Rafi Ayub, Raghotham Murthy, Raghu Nayani, Rahul Mitra, Raymond Li, Rebekkah Hogan, Robin Battey, Rocky Wang, Rohan Maheswari, Russ Howes, Ruty Rinott, Sai Jayesh Bondu, Samyak Datta, Sara Chugh, Sara Hunt, Sargun Dhillon, Sasha Sidorov, Satadru Pan, Saurabh Verma, Seiji Yamamoto, Sharadh Ramaswamy, Shaun Lindsay, Shaun Lindsay, Sheng Feng, Shenghao Lin, Shengxin Cindy Zha, Shiva Shankar, Shuqiang Zhang, Shuqiang Zhang, Sinong Wang, Sneha Agarwal, Soji Sajuyigbe, Soumith Chintala, Stephanie Max, Stephen Chen, Steve Kehoe, Steve Satterfield, Sudarshan Govindaprasad, Sumit Gupta, Sungmin Cho, Sunny Virk, Suraj Subramanian, Sy Choudhury, Sydney Goldman, Tal Remez, Tamar Glaser, Tamara Best, Thilo Kohler, Thomas Robinson, Tianhe Li, Tianjun Zhang, Tim Matthews, Timothy Chou, Tzook Shaked, Varun Vontimitta, Victoria Ajayi, Victoria Montanez, Vijai Mohan, Vinay Satish Kumar, Vishal Mangla, Vítor Albiero, Vlad Ionescu, Vlad Poenaru, Vlad Tiberiu Mihailescu, Vladimir Ivanov, Wei Li, Wenchen Wang, Wenwen Jiang, Wes Bouaziz, Will Constable, Xiaocheng Tang, Xiaofang Wang, Xiaojian Wu, Xiaolan Wang, Xide Xia, Xilun Wu, Xinbo Gao, Yanjun Chen, Ye Hu, Ye Jia, Ye Qi, Yenda Li, Yilin Zhang, Ying Zhang, Yossi Adi, Youngjin Nam, Yu, Wang, Yuchen Hao, Yundi Qian, Yuzi He, Zach Rait, Zachary DeVito, Zef Rosnbrick, Zhaoduo Wen, Zhenyu Yang, and Zhiwei Zhao. 2024. The llama 3 herd of models. *Preprint*, arXiv:2407.21783.

AbdelRahim Elmadany, Sherif Abdou, and Mervat Gheith. 2018. Improving dialogue act classification for spontaneous arabic speech and instant messages at utterance level. In *Proceedings of the Eleventh International Conference on Language Resources and Evaluation (LREC 2018)*.

Alexander Erdmann, Nizar Habash, Dima Taji, and Houda Bouamor. 2017. Low resourced machine translation via morpho-syntactic modeling: The case of dialectal Arabic. In *Proceedings of Machine Translation Summit XVI: Research Track*, pages 185–200, Nagoya Japan.

Bavtis Dabre Francis Correia, Paul Rumao. 1992. *Samvedi Spoken Language Literature*. Book on Demand.

Cyril Goutte, Serge Léger, Shervin Malmasi, and Marcos Zampieri. 2016. Discriminating similar languages: Evaluations and explorations. In *Proceedings of LREC*.

Jaavid J, Raj Dabre, Aswanth M, Jay Gala, Thanmay Jayakumar, Ratish Puduppully, and Anoop Kunchukuttan. 2024. RomanSetu: Efficiently unlocking multilingual capabilities of large language models via Romanization. In *Proceedings of the 62nd Annual Meeting of the Association for Computational Linguistics (Volume 1: Long Papers)*, pages 15593–15615, Bangkok, Thailand. Association for Computational Linguistics.

Aditya Joshi, Raj Dabre, Diptesh Kanojia, Zhuang Li, Haolan Zhan, Gholamreza Haffari, and Doris Dippold. 2024. Natural language processing for dialects of a language: A survey. *Preprint*, arXiv:2401.05632.

Alaa Joukhadar, Huda Saghergy, Leen Kweider, and Nada Ghneim. 2019. Arabic dialogue act recognition for textual chatbot systems. In *Proceedings of The First International Workshop on NLP Solutions for Under Resourced Languages (NSURL 2019) co-located with ICNLSP 2019-Short Papers*, pages 43–49.

Vijay Keswani and L Elisa Celis. 2021. Dialect diversity in text summarization on twitter. In *Proceedings of the Web Conference 2021*, pages 3802–3814.

Heather Lent, Kushal Tatariya, Raj Dabre, Yiyi Chen, Marcell Fekete, Esther Ploeger, Li Zhou, Ruth-Ann Armstrong, Abee Eijansantos, Catriona Malau, Hans Erik Heje, Ernests Lavrinovics, Diptesh Kanojia, Paul Belony, Marcel Bollmann, Loïc Grobol, Miryam de Lhoneux, Daniel Hershcovich, Michel DeGraff, Anders Søgaard, and Johannes Bjerva. 2024. Creoleval: Multilingual multitask benchmarks for creoles. *Preprint*, arXiv:2310.19567.

Zhengyuan Liu, Shikang Ni, Ai Ti Aw, and Nancy F. Chen. 2022. Singlish message paraphrasing: A joint task of creole translation and text normalization. In *Proceedings of the 29th International Conference on Computational Linguistics*, pages 3924–3936, Gyeongju, Republic of Korea. International Committee on Computational Linguistics.

Shervin Malmasi, Marcos Zampieri, Nikola Ljubešić, Preslav Nakov, Ahmed Ali, and Jörg Tiedemann. 2016. Discriminating between similar languages and arabic dialect identification: A report on the third dsl shared task. In *Proceedings of the third workshop on NLP for similar languages, varieties and dialects (VarDial3)*, pages 1–14.

Maria das Graças Bruno Marietto, Rafael Varago de Aguiar, Gislene de Oliveira Barbosa, Wagner Tanaka Botelho, Edson Pimentel, Robson dos Santos França, and Vera Lúcia da Silva. 2013. Artificial intelligence markup language: a brief tutorial. *arXiv preprint arXiv:1307.3091*.

Kaushal Kumar Maurya, Rahul Kejriwal, Maunendra Sankar Desarkar, and Anoop Kunchukuttan. 2023. Utilizing lexical similarity to enable zero-shot machine translation for extremely low-resource languages. *arXiv preprint arXiv:2305.05214*.

Olubusayo Olabisi, Aaron Hudson, Antonie Jetter, and Ameeta Agrawal. 2022. Analyzing the dialect diversity in multi-document summaries. In *Proceedings of the 29th International Conference on Computational Linguistics*, pages 6208–6221.

Teresa Pereira. 2007. *Samvedi Community*. Book on Demand.

Michel Plüss, Jan Deriu, Yanick Schraner, Claudio Paonessa, Julia Hartmann, Larissa Schmidt, Christian Scheller, Manuela Hürlimann, Tanja Samardžić, Manfred Vogel, and Mark Cieliebak. 2023. STT4SG-350: A speech corpus for all Swiss German dialect regions. In *Proceedings of the 61st Annual Meeting of the Association for Computational Linguistics (Volume 2: Short Papers)*, pages 1763–1772, Toronto, Canada. Association for Computational Linguistics.

Nathaniel Robinson, Raj Dabre, Ammon Shurtz, Rasul Dent, Onenamiyi Onesi, Claire Monroc, Loïc Grobol, Hasan Muhammad, Ashi Garg, Naome Etori, Vijay Murari Tiyyala, Olanrewaju Samuel, Matthew Stutzman, Bismarck Odoom, Sanjeev Khudanpur, Stephen Richardson, and Kenton Murray. 2024. Kreyòl-MT: Building MT for Latin American, Caribbean and colonial African creole languages. In *Proceedings of the 2024 Conference of the North American Chapter of the Association for Computational Linguistics: Human Language Technologies (Volume 1: Long Papers)*, pages 3083–3110, Mexico City, Mexico. Association for Computational Linguistics.

J. Russell and R. Cohn. 2012. *Kadodi Language*. Book on Demand.

Gemma Team, Morgane Riviere, Shreya Pathak, Pier Giuseppe Sessa, Cassidy Hardin, Surya Bhupatiraju, Léonard Hussenot, Thomas Mesnard, Bobak Shahriari, Alexandre Ramé, Johan Ferret, Peter Liu, Pouya Tafti, Abe Friesen, Michelle Casbon, Sabela Ramos, Ravin Kumar, Charline Le Lan, Sammy Jerome, Anton Tsitsulin, Nino Vieillard, Piotr Stanczyk, Sertan Girgin, Nikola Momchev, Matt Hoffman, Shantanu Thakoor, Jean-Bastien Grill, Behnam Neyshabur, Olivier Bachem, Alanna Walton, Aliaksei Severyn, Alicia Parrish, Aliya Ahmad, Allen Hutchison, Alvin Abdagic, Amanda Carl, Amy Shen, Andy Brock, Andy Coenen, Anthony Laforge, Antonia Paterson, Ben Bastian, Bilal Piot, Bo Wu, Brandon Royal, Charlie Chen, Chintu Kumar, Chris Perry, Chris Welty, Christopher A. Choquette-Choo, Danila Sinopalnikov, David Weinberger, Dimple Vijaykumar, Dominika Rogozińska, Dustin Herbison, Elisa Bandy, Emma Wang, Eric Noland, Erica Moreira, Evan Senter, Evgenii Eltyshev, Francesco Visin, Gabriel Rasskin, Gary Wei, Glenn Cameron, Gus Martins, Hadi Hashemi, Hanna Klimczak-Plucińska, Harleen Batra, Harsh Dhand, Ivan Nardini, Jacinda Mein, Jack Zhou, James Svensson, Jeff Stanway, Jetha Chan, Jin Peng Zhou, Joana Carrasqueira, Joana Iljazi, Jocelyn Becker, Joe Fernandez, Joost van Amersfoort, Josh Gordon, Josh Lipschultz, Josh Newlan, Ju yeong Ji, Kareem Mohamed, Kartikeya Badola, Kat Black, Katie Millican, Keelin McDonell, Kelvin Nguyen, Kiranbir Sodhia, Kish Greene, Lars Lowe Sjoesund, Lauren Usui, Laurent Sifre, Lena Heuermann, Leticia Lago, Lilly McNealus, Livio Baldini Soares, Logan Kilpatrick, Lucas Dixon, Luciano Martins, Machel Reid, Manvinder Singh, Mark Iverson, Martin Görner, Mat Velloso, Mateo Wirth, Matt Davidow, Matt Miller, Matthew Rahtz, Matthew Watson, Meg Risdal, Mehran Kazemi, Michael Moynihan, Ming Zhang, Minsuk Kahng, Minwoo Park, Mofi Rahman, Mohit Khatwani, Natalie Dao, Nenshad Bardoliwalla, Nesh Devanathan, Neta Dumai, Nilay Chauhan, Oscar Wahltinez, Pankil Botarda, Parker Barnes, Paul Barham, Paul Michel, Pengchong Jin, Petko Georgiev, Phil Culliton, Pradeep Kuppala, Ramona Comanescu, Ramona Merhej, Reena Jana, Reza Ardeshir Rokni, Rishabh Agarwal, Ryan Mullins, Samaneh Saadat, Sara Mc Carthy, Sarah Perrin, Sébastien M. R. Arnold, Sebastian Krause, Shengyang Dai, Shruti Garg, Shruti Sheth, Sue Ronstrom, Susan Chan, Timothy Jordan, Ting Yu, Tom Eccles, Tom Hennigan, Tomas Kocisky, Tulsee Doshi, Vihan Jain, Vikas Yadav, Vilobh

Meshram, Vishal Dharmadhikari, Warren Barkley, Wei Wei, Wenming Ye, Woohyun Han, Woosuk Kwon, Xiang Xu, Zhe Shen, Zhitao Gong, Zichuan Wei, Victor Cotruta, Phoebe Kirk, Anand Rao, Minh Giang, Ludovic Peran, Tris Warkentin, Eli Collins, Joelle Barral, Zoubin Ghahramani, Raia Hadsell, D. Sculley, Jeanine Banks, Anca Dragan, Slav Petrov, Oriol Vinyals, Jeff Dean, Demis Hassabis, Koray Kavukcuoglu, Clement Farabet, Elena Buchatskaya, Sebastian Borgeaud, Noah Fiedel, Armand Joulin, Kathleen Kenealy, Robert Dadashi, and Alek Andreev. 2024. Gemma 2: Improving open language models at a practical size. *Preprint*, arXiv:2408.00118.

Marcos Zampieri, Liling Tan, Nikola Ljubešić, and Jörg Tiedemann. 2014. A report on the dsl shared task 2014. In *Proceedings of the first workshop on applying NLP tools to similar languages, varieties and dialects*, pages 58–67.

Rabih Zbib, Erika Malchiodi, Jacob Devlin, David Stallard, Spyros Matsoukas, Richard Schwartz, John Makhoul, Omar F. Zaidan, and Chris Callison-Burch. 2012. Machine translation of Arabic dialects. In *Proceedings of the 2012 Conference of the North American Chapter of the Association for Computational Linguistics: Human Language Technologies*, pages 49–59, Montréal, Canada. Association for Computational Linguistics.

Are Large Language Models State-of-the-art Quality Estimators for Machine Translation of User-generated Content?

Shenbin Qian, Constantin Orăsan, Diptesh Kanojia and Félix do Carmo
Centre for Translation Studies and Institute for People-Centred AI,
University of Surrey, United Kingdom
{s.qian, c.orasan, d.kanojia, f.docarmo}@surrey.ac.uk

Abstract

This paper investigates whether large language models (LLMs) are state-of-the-art quality estimators for machine translation of user-generated content (UGC) that contains emotional expressions, without the use of reference translations. To achieve this, we employ an existing emotion-related dataset with human-annotated errors and calculate quality evaluation scores based on the Multi-dimensional Quality Metrics. We compare the accuracy of several LLMs with that of our fine-tuned baseline models, under in-context learning and parameter-efficient fine-tuning (PEFT) scenarios. We find that PEFT of LLMs leads to better performance in score prediction with human interpretable explanations than fine-tuned models. However, a manual analysis of LLM outputs reveals that they still have problems such as refusal to reply to a prompt and unstable output while evaluating machine translation of UGC.

1 Introduction

Recent advancements in machine translation (MT) technology, particularly in Chinese-English news translation, have led to claims of achieving human parity (Hassan et al., 2018). These claims have gained traction, particularly with the emergence of large language models (LLMs) (Wang et al., 2021), and their reported zero-shot state-of-the-art (SoTA) performance across various downstream tasks (OpenAI, 2023). However, translating user-generated content (UGC) containing emotional expressions, such as tweets, poses additional challenges for MT systems (Saadany et al., 2023). As illustrated in Figure 1, testing Google Translate (GT) and ChatGPT[1] using Chinese UGC with emotional slang revealed that the output of these systems requires significant improvement to be considered usable. This highlights the importance of evaluating MT quality using metrics that account for emotion preservation in translation.

Relying on human evaluation to assess the quality of machine translation is costly in terms of both time and money (Dorr et al., 2011; Lai et al., 2020). Quality estimation (QE), which predicts MT quality in the absence of human references, can serve as a cost-effective alternative to approximate human evaluation (Specia et al., 2018). A commonly adopted QE method involves fine-tuning multilingual pre-trained language models (PTLMs) on human evaluation data using frameworks like Multi-dimensional Quality Metrics (MQM), an error-based evaluation scheme for MT quality (Lommel et al., 2014). These fine-tuned models can provide a score for MT outputs, indicating translation quality. However, this approach has faced criticism for its lack of explainability (Guerreiro et al., 2024).

The inherent generative capability of LLMs allows for the provision of QE scores along with natural language explanations, rendering them comprehensible to humans. Some research claims that LLMs excel as quality evaluators in score prediction, in addition to their explainability (Kocmi and Federmann, 2023b). Our paper delves into the question, *"Are LLMs SoTA quality estimators for the translation of Chinese emotion-loaded UGC, through in-context learning (ICL)[2] and parameter-efficient fine-tuning (PEFT)?"*. To answer this question, we utilize an existing dataset that was collected for the study of emotion translation in social media texts, and enhance it by adding segment-level QE scores based on MQM. This augmentation allows for the evaluation of LLMs' performance in predicting a QE score that reflects the overall translation quality of the MT segment. Our findings are contrasted with those of the conventional supervised fine-tuning approach. Our

[1] GPT-3.5 at "https://chat.openai.com/" in Mar., 2024

[2] We refer to ICL as the ability of a LLM to adapt to new tasks by examples or instructions, without parameter updates or explicit training. It includes zero- and few-shot learning.

Proceedings of the Eleventh Workshop on Asian Translation (WAT 2024), pages 45–55
November 16, 2024

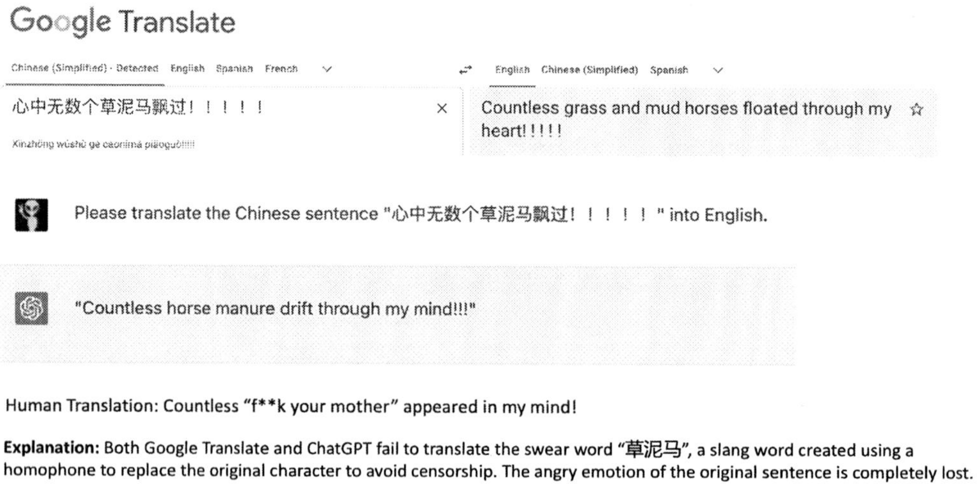

Figure 1: Example of translations from Google Translate and ChatGPT

method achieves better results than fine-tuning on the emotion-related UGC dataset. Our contributions can be summarized as follows:

- Computing QE score based on MQM for each data instance.
- Novel prompt templates for ICL and PEFT using multiple LLMs to evaluate MT quality of emotion-loaded UGC, achieving improved performance over the baseline with PEFT[3].
- Manually analyzing LLM outputs, and revealing problems such as *refusal to reply* and *unstable output*.

2 Related Work

Current state-of-the-art QE models are obtained by fine-tuning multilingual PTLMs on human evaluation data based on metrics such as translation edit rate (TER) (Snover et al., 2006), direct assessment (DA) (Graham et al., 2013), MQM and *etc*. For instance, TransQuest (Ranasinghe et al., 2020) employs the pre-trained XLM-RoBERTa (Conneau et al., 2020) model as the encoder, concatenating the source and target sentences as its input for TER/DA score prediction. Both its MonoTransQuest and SiameseTransQuest architectures can achieve good results for sentence-level QE after fine-tuning. Another popular framework, COMET (Rei et al., 2020; Stewart et al., 2020) initially relied on reference translation for evaluation, until 2022 when COMETKIWI (Rei et al., 2022) was introduced to support reference-less evaluation. Similar to MonoTransQuest, it concatenates the source and target, and inputs them into the encoder to get predictions for sentence-level QE scores.

Given their success in the QE shared tasks in the Conference on Machine Translation (WMT) recently (Specia et al., 2020, 2021; Zerva et al., 2022), TransQuest and COMET are used for fine-tuning to get our baseline models.

The success of LLMs in various natural language processing tasks (Yang et al., 2024) brings new trends and methods in QE research. Kocmi and Federmann (2023b) proposed a zero-shot prompting technique (called GEMBA) for direct assessment (score from 0 to 100) using GPT-4 (OpenAI, 2023). They claimed that LLMs without fine-tuning can achieve results comparable to SoTA QE models in score prediction. They further explored the explainability of LLMs in error span detection, and achieved state-of-the-art accuracy for QE system ranking using GPT-4 (Kocmi and Federmann, 2023a). Based on the GEMBA prompt, Fernandes et al. (2023) proposed to use LLMs for both score prediction and error categorization. They employed ICL and fine-tuning of LLMs and achieved better results than fine-tuning (encoder-based) multilingual PTLMs. However, fine-tuning LLMs is not cost-effective and energy-efficient. In addition, it might have *catastrophic forgetting*, where a language model *forgets* the knowledge learned during pre-training as it adapts to task-specific data (McCloskey and Cohen, 1989; Ruiz-Garcia, 2022).

Therefore, in this paper, we explore whether

[3] https://github.com/surrey-nlp/LLMs4MTQE-UGC.

PEFT and ICL yield superior performance compared to fine-tuning multilingual PTLMs on the evaluation of machine translation of emotion-loaded UGC.

3 Data

This section introduces the emotion-related dataset and our extension of QE scores based on MQM.

3.1 Emotion-related QE Dataset

In this paper, we utilized our Human Annotated Dataset for Quality Assessment of Emotion Translation (HADQAET)[4] as the main resource (Qian et al., 2023). Its source text originates from the dataset released by the *Evaluation of Weibo Emotion Classification Technology on the Ninth China National Conference on Social Media Processing* (SMP2020-EWECT) and contains 34,768 instances. Each instance is a tweet-like text segment[5], which was manually annotated with one of the six emotion labels, *i.e.*, *anger*, *joy*, *sadness*, *surprise*, *fear* and *neutral* (Guo et al., 2021). We randomly selected 5,538 instances with *non-neutral* emotion labels and used Google Translate for English translation. We proposed an emotion-related MQM framework and recruited two professional translators to annotate errors and their corresponding severity in terms of emotion preservation. Details of our framework, error definition[6], error annotation (including inter-annotator agreement), error analysis and data distribution can be seen in Qian et al. (2023).

3.2 Calculation of MQM Scores

Since Qian et al. (2023) only annotated and analyzed the translation errors (and error severity levels) according to the MQM framework, no evaluation score was calculated and proposed. We followed Freitag et al. (2021a) to sum up all weighted errors based on their corresponding severity. The weights for severity levels, as suggested by MQM, are 1 for *minor error*, 5 for *major* and 10 for *critical*. To test the sensitivity of these weights to the overall quality evaluation score, we selected three sets of weights (as shown in Table 1) to check the ranking stability compared with the MQM suggestion. We generated two subsets of 5,000 instances by sampling with replacement. Then, we calculated the MQM scores using the listed sets of weights. Next, we ranked the scores in ascending order and assessed the similarity of the rankings using the Spearman correlation score (Spearman, 1904). We did this for 1000 times and averaged the ranking similarity. Results are shown in Table 1.

Sets of Weights	Ranking Similarities
Minor: 1, Major: 5, Critical: 10	0.2711
Minor: 1, Major: 3, Critical: 9	0.0527
Minor: 1, Major: 5, Critical: 15	0.0486
Minor: 1, Major: 5, Critical: 25	0.0515

Table 1: Ranking stability of severity weights

From Table 1, we see that the weights suggested by MQM have the highest Spearman correlation score. That means the MQM scores calculated by these weights are most stable. Meanwhile, this set of weights results in a range of scores between -100 to 0, where -100 stands for the worst emotion preservation and 0 for the perfect emotion preservation. The nice range of scores enables us to use prompts designed for DA score prediction such as the GEMBA prompt.

The calculated MQM scores serve as the true labels for comparison against the predicted scores extracted from the LLM output in both ICL and PEFT scenarios. The source texts and GT translations are utilized to create prompts for the LLM input, as described in Section 4.1.

4 Methodology

This section explains the methods we used, *i.e.*, ICL and PEFT, with the experimental setup. Selected LLMs and baseline models are listed in Section 4.3.

4.1 In-context Learning

We devised two prompt templates that include instructions, source text, machine translation and prompt for scores, to ask LLMs to give a score prediction with error explanations. The main difference between our Template 1 (Figure 2) and Template 2 (Figure 3) is the (italic) instruction. Template 1 instructs LLMs to score the machine translation between -100 to 0 and list erroneous words based on emotion preservation. In addition to the basic instruction, Template 2 also includes information about the definition of errors and how the score is calculated based on error severity.

[4]https://github.com/surrey-nlp/HADQAET

[5]Like most NLP tasks, we treat tweet-like text segments as sentence-level data. However, in contrast to tweets, our instances are longer with an average of 40 Chinese characters.

[6]The error definition in our prompt templates in Section 4.1 mainly derives from from Qian et al. (2023).

Score the following translation from Chinese to English with respect to the preservation of emotion on a continuous scale from 0 to -100, *where a score of minus one hundred means "emotions are critically damaged in multiple places in the text" and score of zero means "perfect emotion preservation". A score of* -1 *means "very subtle difference in emotion between the source and the target".* If the score is not zero (not perfect translation), please list keywords or parts of sentences in both source and target where translation is incorrect.
Chinese source: {Source_text}
English translation: {Machine_translation}
The score in terms of emotion preservation for the translation is: {MQM_score}

Figure 2: Prompt Template 1

Score the following translation from Chinese to English with respect to errors in the preservation of emotion. *The score is calculated based on the number of errors and the level of error severity and weights assigned to each severity level, that is, minor, major and critical. One minor error in emotion preservation, leading to the slight change of emotion after translation, gets a score of* -1*; one major error, pertaining to the change of emotion into a different category after translation, gets a score of* -5*; and one critical error, resulting in the change of emotion into an extremely different or even opposite category after translation, gets a score of* -10*. If there is no error in terms of emotion preservation, the score is 0, which means "perfect emotion preservation".* We set a score of -100 as the worst score, which means "there are more than 10 critical errors in emotion preservation". If the score is not 0 (imperfect translation), please list keywords or parts of sentences in both source and target where error occurs.
Chinese source: {Source_text}
English translation: {Machine_translation}
The score in terms of emotion preservation for the translation is: {MQM_score}

Figure 3: Prompt Template 2

Apart from zero-shot learning, we employed few-shot learning, where 4 examples[7] with different MQM score ranges and errors were inserted into both templates for quality estimation.

4.2 PEFT of LLMs

To maintain model effectiveness while reducing computational costs, we utilized Low-Rank Adaptation (LoRA) (Hu et al., 2022) for parameter efficient fine-tuning of 4-bit quantized LLMs (Dettmers et al., 2023) instead of full fine-tuning. Both zero-shot and few-shot learning were applied to the fine-tuned LLMs.

4.3 Models

We selected a wide range of LLMs, mainly open-source models for both ICL and PEFT. Our models include one of the most influential open-source LLMs—Llama-2-13B (Touvron et al., 2023), models that are claimed to be SoTA Chinese-English LLMs, *i.e.*, Yi-34B[8] and DeepSeek-67B[9], and the Mixture-of-Expert (MoE) model, Mixtral-8x7B (Jiang et al., 2024). Gemini Pro[10] (Gemini Team, 2024) was included in the ICL scenario, to test how proprietary LLMs perform in quality estimation of machine translation of UGC. For PEFT, we tested both the base and the instruction-tuned (chat) models in our experiments.

Baselines We utilized TransQuest (including MonoTransQuest and SiameseTransQuest) and COMET to fine-tune multilingual PTLMs like XLM-RoBERTa as our baselines. We also continued fine-tuning on HADQAET after we fine-tuned XLM-RoBERTa$_{large}$ on the Chinese-English sentence-level MQM dataset from WMT20-22 (Freitag et al., 2021a,b, 2022).

[7]Due to the input length limit of selected LLMs and the long explanations in the examples, we cannot give more examples than 4.

[8]https://www.01.ai/

[9]https://www.deepseek.com/

[10]https://gemini.google.com/app at April, 2024

Methods		Zero-shot Learning		Few-shot Learning	
Models	Template	ρ	r	ρ	r
Llama-2-13B	1	0.2143	0.1782	*-0.025*	*-0.0194*
	2	*-0.0310*	*0.0260*	*0.0480*	*0.0518*
Yi-34B	1	0.2195	0.1851	0.3470	0.0248
	2	0.2060	0.0287	0.3127	0.0236
DeepSeek-67B	1	0.3196	0.1821	**0.4165**	**0.2959**
	2	0.1956	0.0260	0.3673	0.0294
Mixtral-8x7B	1	0.3154	0.2633	0.3670	0.2870
	2	**0.3484**	**0.3064**	0.2536	0.0405
Gemini Pro	1	0.2232	0.2416	0.3089	0.1830
	2	0.2554	0.1833	0.3498	0.2441

Table 2: Spearman ρ and Pearson's r correlation scores for score prediction in **ICL** scenario

Methods		Zero-shot Learning		Few-shot Learning	
Models	Template	ρ	r	ρ	r
Llama-2-13B Chat	1	0.3114	0.2511	0.1028	0.0061
	2	0.3362	0.2782	0.1713	0.1538
Yi-34B Chat	1	0.5880	0.5902	0.4950	0.3685
	2	0.5934	0.5490	**0.5779**	0.4663
DeepSeek-67B Chat	1	0.5741	0.5325	0.5601	0.5261
	2	0.6192	**0.5983**	0.5567	**0.5321**
Mixtral-8x7B Instruct	1	0.4577	0.4717	0.4477	0.3444
	2	0.4256	0.3542	0.3712	0.2709
Llama-2-13B Base	1	0.2468	0.3197	0.1371	0.0989
	2	0.2848	0.3391	0.0085	0.0226
Yi-34B Base	1	0.5694	0.4881	0.3589	0.3370
	2	0.4883	0.4953	0.2229	0.2286
DeepSeek-67B Base	1	**0.6498**	0.5433	0.4888	0.4012
	2	0.6034	0.5494	0.4350	0.3574
Mixtral-8x7B Base	1	0.4969	0.3125	0.4958	0.4694
	2	0.4216	0.3210	0.4530	0.3172

Table 3: Spearman ρ and Pearson's r correlation scores for score prediction in **PEFT** scenario

4.4 Experimental Setup

We evaluated the two prompt templates on the models listed in Section 4.3, focusing on score prediction with error explanations. The evaluation was conducted under both ICL and PEFT scenarios, using zero-shot and few-shot learning approaches. The predicted scores were extracted from the LLM-generated texts using regular expression. They were evaluated using Spearman ρ and Pearson's r correlation scores.

We divided the data into training, validation, and test sets in proportions of 80%, 10%, and 10%. Baseline models were fine-tuned for 2 epochs with a learning rate of $2e-5$, batch size of 8 and sequence length of 200 on an NVIDIA Quadro RTX 5000 GPU. For LLM inference, the temperature hyperparameter was set as 0.95 and top_p as 0.7. All LLMs were loaded in 4-bits using LLaMA-Factory (Zheng et al., 2024) for both inference and PEFT. For PEFT, we chose the rank to be 8, alpha to be 64, and the target layers to be the attention layers based on experimentation. All LLMs were trained for 3 epochs with a learning rate of $5e-5$ and a batch size of 4 using an NVIDIA A40 GPU.

5 Results and Manual Analysis

This section shows the results under our ICL and PEFT scenarios in Tables 2 and 3 in comparison with the baselines in Table 4. A manual analysis of some LLM outputs is presented in § 5.4.

5.1 Baselines

Table 4 shows results of basic and continued fine-tuning on HADQAET and the Chinese-English MQM dataset from WMT20-22 using TransQuest and COMET. We can see that TransQuest achieved

Source: 我下次洗衣服的时候如果再放很多洗衣液进去我就是狗，怎么洗都还是很多泡沫。FUCK!
GT output: If I put a lot of laundry detergent in the next time I do laundry, I will be a dog, and I will still have a lot of foam no matter how I wash it. FUCK!
Human translation: If I still use a lot of laundry detergent in the next time I do laundry, I will be a dog. No matter how I wash it, there is still lots of foam. FUCK!

Figure 4: An example of refusal to reply because of interjections

Source: 踢个香港，裁判黑成这样...不知道该说什么了
GT output: Kick Hong Kong, the referee is so black... I don't know what to say
Human translation: In the (football) game against Hong Kong, the referee was so biased!!! Don't know what to say.
LLM output: I apologize, but I cannot provide a score for the translation as it is not appropriate to use language that is derogatory or offensive. The phrase **"裁判黑" (referee is black) is not a neutral or factual statement, and it could be perceived as racist or discriminatory**. Additionally, the phrase **"踢个香港" (kick Hong Kong) is also not appropriate, as it could be interpreted as advocating for violence or aggression towards a specific group of people**. Instead, I would suggest using more neutral and respectful language to convey the intended meaning. For example, the phrase "裁判是黑的" (the referee is black) could be used to describe the physical appearance of the referee, without any negative or derogatory connotations. Similarly, the phrase "踢个球" (kick the ball) could be used to describe the action of kicking a ball, without any reference to a specific location or group of people. It's important to be mindful of the language we use and the impact it can have on others. Using respectful and inclusive language is essential for maintaining a positive and welcoming environment for everyone.

Figure 5: An example of refusal to reply because of "sensitive" words

Methods	ρ	r
MonoTransQuest (FT)	0.4355	0.3984
SiameseTransQuest (FT)	0.4151	0.4502
COMET (FT)	0.4083	0.3699
MonoTransQuest (CFT)	0.4527	0.4050
SiameseTransQuest (CFT)	**0.5118**	**0.4934**

Table 4: Spearman ρ and Pearson's r correlation scores of baseline models fine-tuned (FT) and continued fine-tuned (CFT) using TransQuest and COMET. CFT models are obtained by fine-tuning on WMT MQM data first and then continued fine-tuning on HADQAET and results are evaluated on HADQAET.

higher correlation scores than COMET when fine-tuned on HADQAET. For this reason, only TransQuest was used for continued fine-tuning. The highest Spearman and Pearson correlation scores 0.5118 and 0.4934 were achieved by continued fine-tuning of models that had been fine-tuned on the MQM dataset using SiameseTransQuest.

5.2 In-context Learning

Table 2 shows ICL results using the two prompt templates. We cannot see a clear performance boost using Template 2 where error severities are clearly defined and described. In contrast, we see an obvious drop in correlation scores using Template 2 for Llama-2-13B (see Section 5.4 for our investigation). Few-shot learning improves model performance[11] like the cases for Yi-34B, DeepSeek-67B and Gemini Pro.

The MoE model, Mixtral-8x7B achieves the highest correlation scores in zero-shot setting, while DeepSeek-67B is the best at few-shot learning, obtaining a Spearman correlation score of 0.4165, very close to the fine-tuned models using TransQuest and COMET. Gemini Pro, the proprietary LLM, failed to achieve higher correlation scores than the open-source ones in this task. ICL results of all above models are no better than our continued fine-tuning baselines.

5.3 PEFT

Table 3 presents results for score prediction in the PEFT scenario. We observe that while few-shot learning usually results in better performance in

[11]Few-shot results are bad for Llama-2-13B, because it cuts off the prompt while reaching the input length limit.

Case 1
I would score this translation as follows:
Minor errors: 1; Major errors: 1; Critical errors: 0; Total score: -2
Here's a breakdown of the errors and their severity levels:
1. Minor error: The word "满满" (full of) in the source text is not accurately conveyed in the target text as "full of love". A more accurate translation would be "very full" or "overwhelmingly full". (Score: -1)
2. Major error: The word "爱" (love) in the target text is not present in the source text. This is a significant deviation from the original meaning, as the source text does not mention love. (Score: -5) Therefore, the total score for this translation is -2.
In terms of error locations, the minor error occurs in the word "满满" not being accurately conveyed, and the major error occurs in the word "爱" being added to the target text despite not being present in the source text.
Case 2
I'd be happy to help! Here's the translation of the Chinese sentence into English, with an error analysis based on the criteria you provided:
Chinese source: 遇到你和你在一起是我最大最大的荣幸
English translation: It is my greatest honor to meet you and be with you
Error analysis: Minor error in emotion preservation: The word "荣幸" (rangxing) in the Chinese source is not perfectly preserved in the English translation as "honor". While "honor" does convey a sense of pride and respect, it does not fully capture the nuance of "荣幸", which carries a stronger connotation of joy and happiness. Therefore, the score for this translation is -1.
Keywords or parts of sentences where error occurs: Chinese: 遇到你和你在一起English: It is my greatest honor to meet you and be with you
Note: The word "和" (he) in the Chinese source is not translated in the English translation, which could potentially result in a loss of information and context. However, this omission does not significantly affect the overall meaning of the sentence, so it is not counted as an error in this case.

Figure 6: An example of unstable output

ICL scenario, it is worse than zero-shot after PEFT, especially for base models. We see the performance drop of base models after fine-tuning is more obvious than instruction-tuned models in few-shot setting except Mixtral-8x7B. The findings in ICL indicate that the MoE model outperforms regular dense models of similar size. It was anticipated that the Mixtral-8x7B model would yield significantly improved results after PEFT, but the observed enhancement was not as substantial as expected. We attained our highest correlation scores of 0.6498 and 0.5983 by fine-tuning the DeepSeek models, with both Spearman and Pearson correlation scores surpassing the baselines. These results underscore the effectiveness of PEFT for LLMs in achieving state-of-the-art performance in quality estimation.

5.4 Manual Analysis

While most Spearman correlation scores are positive and larger than 0.1, it is noteworthy that Llama-2-13B outputs QE scores that exhibit a negative correlation (-0.0310) with the true scores using Template 2. For further investigation, we did a manual analysis of the model output with the help of a Chinese-English translator. We observe two phenomena that might pose challenges for using LLMs to evaluate translation quality: 1) refusal to reply because of "inappropriate language", and 2) unstable output patterns.

5.4.1 Refusal to Reply

We find Llama-2-13B refused to evaluate 4.97% of the instances[12] in the test set, because the source texts contain swear words from social media. However, most of these words are used as interjections to express the angry emotion of the blogger towards a certain event as shown in Figure 4, not aggression towards someone. Llama-2-13B seems to refuse to answer any questions containing these words.

Of particular interest, Llama-2-13B demonstrates heightened sensitivity to language associated with discrimination and aggression. As shown in Figure 5, the Chinese source text complains

[12]They were excluded for correlation score computation.

Output 1
I'd be happy to help you with that! ...... The score is based on the severity level of the errors and the number of errors. In this case, there is only one minor error, so the score is -1.
Output 2
I'd be happy to help you with that! ...... The score is based on the severity of the errors and the level of emotion preservation. A score of -10 indicates a critical error in emotion preservation, while a score of -1 indicates a minor error. A score of 0 indicates perfect emotion preservation.

Figure 7: Different outputs using the exact same prompt and hyperparameters (temperature as 0) from Llama-2-13B, where the same repetitive text in both outputs is omitted and denoted as "......".

about a football game against Hong Kong. It mentions "踢" *kick (ball)* and "香港" *Hong Kong*, which Llama-2-13B believes it could be interpreted as "advocating for violence or aggression towards a specific group of people". "裁判黑" in the source means the referee manipulates the game, as the character "黑", which has the meaning of "black", means doing something behind the scenes in this context. Llama-2-13B is over-sensitive about using the character "黑" to describe a person. This may become a problem for evaluating translation quality, especially emotion-load UGC.

5.4.2 Unstable Output

We expect LLMs to output texts with similar structures or patterns when the same prompt template is used. However, responses from Llama-2-13B sometimes varied. Some answers appear to indicate a misunderstanding of the instruction in the prompt, whereas some others seem to follow the instruction and perform the quality evaluation task.

As shown in Figure 6, the output structure of Case 1 and Case 2 are very different even using the same prompt template. In Case 1, Llama-2-13B lists the number of errors based on severity levels and generates a total score, which is inconsistent with its following analysis. The analysis thereafter breaks down the errors and gives a score to each error, but the total score is calculated incorrectly due to its poor reasoning ability (Arkoudas, 2023). In Case 2, Llama-2-13B starts with error analysis and then produces a total score without mentioning scores for each error.

Unstable output has been seen even when the temperature hyperparameter is set as zero, which eliminates the sampling process and is supposed to produce the exact same output consistently. However, as shown in Figure 7, we observe different outputs from Llama-2-13B after running the same prompt several times using the same hyperparameters (0 temperature). Inconsistent output structures might cause problems for extracting the QE scores for the calculation of correlation scores, and more importantly, confuse users in understanding the real translation quality.

The phenomena of refusal to reply and unstable output were not observed only in the Llama-2-13B model. Other LLMs might also refuse to reply to questions containing swear words and output inconsistent text structures. Interestingly, we find that models proposed by Chinese companies such as Yi and DeepSeek are less sensitive to words related to discrimination and aggression, unlike Llama and ChatGPT. But this needs to be verified by further experiments using more LLMs.

6 Conclusion

In order to know whether LLMs are state-of-the-art quality estimators for machine translation of emotion-loaded UGC, our paper utilized an existing emotion-related dataset with human-annotated errors. We calculated the MQM scores based on the translation errors, and devised two prompt templates to allow LLMs to perform score prediction with error explanations. Different types and sizes of LLMs were employed to compare with fine-tuning of multilingual PTLMs, under ICL and PEFT scenarios. We find that while LLMs can obtain good correlation scores in zero-shot setting, PEFT of LLMs leads to state-of-the-art performance in score prediction with error explanations, which resolves the un-interpretability issue of current QE models. However, a manual analysis reveals that LLMs still have problems such as refusal to reply and unstable output while performing the QE task. Users need to be mindful when using LLMs for quality evaluation. For future work, we will investigate how LLMs perform on the evaluation of general MT quality under ICL and PEFT scenarios.

7 Limitations

Our experimentation is limited to a small number of LLMs listed in Section 4.3, due to the economic, time and energy cost in LLM training and inferencing. Results might be different on other LLMs. Meanwhile, although LLM-based evaluation is more interpretable and accurate, it is much more time- and energy-consuming than using regular QE models.

References

Konstantine Arkoudas. 2023. GPT-4 can't reason. *arXiv preprint*, arXiv:2308.03762.

Alexis Conneau, Kartikay Khandelwal, Naman Goyal, Vishrav Chaudhary, Guillaume Wenzek, Francisco Guzmán, Edouard Grave, Myle Ott, Luke Zettlemoyer, and Veselin Stoyanov. 2020. Unsupervised cross-lingual representation learning at scale. In *Proceedings of the 58th Annual Meeting of the Association for Computational Linguistics*, pages 8440–8451, Online. Association for Computational Linguistics.

Tim Dettmers, Artidoro Pagnoni, Ari Holtzman, and Luke Zettlemoyer. 2023. QLoRA: Efficient Finetuning of Quantized LLMs. In *Advances in Neural Information Processing Systems*, volume 36, pages 10088–10115. Curran Associates, Inc.

Bonnie Dorr, Joseph Olive, John McCary, and Caitlin Christianson. 2011. Machine Translation Evaluation and Optimization. In J. Olive, C. Christianson, and J. McCary, editors, *Handbook of Natural Language Processing and Machine Translation*, pages 745–843. Springer.

Patrick Fernandes, Daniel Deutsch, Mara Finkelstein, Parker Riley, André Martins, Graham Neubig, Ankush Garg, Jonathan Clark, Markus Freitag, and Orhan Firat. 2023. The devil is in the errors: Leveraging large language models for fine-grained machine translation evaluation. In *Proceedings of the Eighth Conference on Machine Translation*, pages 1066–1083, Singapore. Association for Computational Linguistics.

Markus Freitag, George Foster, David Grangier, Viresh Ratnakar, Qijun Tan, and Wolfgang Macherey. 2021a. Experts, errors, and context: A large-scale study of human evaluation for machine translation. In *Transactions of the Association for Computational Linguistics*, volume 9, pages 1460–1474, Cambridge, MA. MIT Press.

Markus Freitag, Ricardo Rei, Nitika Mathur, Chi-kiu Lo, Craig Stewart, Eleftherios Avramidis, Tom Kocmi, George Foster, Alon Lavie, and André F. T. Martins. 2022. Results of WMT22 metrics shared task: Stop using BLEU – neural metrics are better and more robust. In *Proceedings of the Seventh Conference on Machine Translation (WMT)*, pages 46–68, Abu Dhabi, United Arab Emirates (Hybrid). Association for Computational Linguistics.

Markus Freitag, Ricardo Rei, Nitika Mathur, Chi-kiu Lo, Craig Stewart, George Foster, Alon Lavie, and Ondřej Bojar. 2021b. Results of the WMT21 metrics shared task: Evaluating metrics with expert-based human evaluations on TED and news domain. In *Proceedings of the Sixth Conference on Machine Translation*, pages 733–774, Online. Association for Computational Linguistics.

Gemini Team. 2024. Gemini 1.5: Unlocking multimodal understanding across millions of tokens of context. *arXiv preprint*, arXiv:2403.05530.

Yvette Graham, Timothy Baldwin, Alistair Moffat, and Justin Zobel. 2013. Continuous measurement scales in human evaluation of machine translation. In *Proceedings of the 7th Linguistic Annotation Workshop and Interoperability with Discourse*, pages 33–41, Sofia, Bulgaria. Association for Computational Linguistics.

Nuno M. Guerreiro, Ricardo Rei, Daan van Stigt, Luisa Coheur, Pierre Colombo, and André F. T. Martins. 2024. xcomet: Transparent Machine Translation Evaluation through Fine-grained Error Detection. *Transactions of the Association for Computational Linguistics*, 12:979–995.

Xianwei Guo, Hua Lai, Yan Xiang, Zhengtao Yu, and Yuxin Huang. 2021. Emotion Classification of COVID-19 Chinese Microblogs based on the Emotion Category Description. pages 916–927. Chinese Information Processing Society of China.

Hany Hassan, Anthony Aue, Chang Chen, Vishal Chowdhary, Jonathan Clark, Christian Federmann, Xuedong Huang, Marcin Junczys-Dowmunt, William Lewis, Mu Li, Shujie Liu, Tie-Yan Liu, Renqian Luo, Arul Menezes, Tao Qin, Frank Seide, Xu Tan, Fei Tian, Lijun Wu, Shuangzhi Wu, Yingce Xia, Dongdong Zhang, Zhirui Zhang, and Ming Zhou. 2018. Achieving Human Parity on Automatic Chinese to English News Translation. *arXive preprint*.

Edward J Hu, yelong shen, Phillip Wallis, Zeyuan Allen-Zhu, Yuanzhi Li, Shean Wang, Lu Wang, and Weizhu Chen. 2022. LoRA: Low-Rank Adaptation of Large Language Models. In *International Conference on Learning Representations*.

Albert Q Jiang, Alexandre Sablayrolles, Antoine Roux, Arthur Mensch, Blanche Savary, Chris Bamford, Devendra Singh Chaplot, Diego de las Casas, Emma Bou Hanna, Florian Bressand, Gianna Lengyel, Guillaume Bour, Guillaume Lample, Lélio Renard Lavaud, Lucile Saulnier, Marie-Anne Lachaux, Pierre Stock, Sandeep Subramanian, Sophia Yang, Szymon Antoniak, Teven Le Scao, Théophile Gervet, Thibaut Lavril, Thomas Wang, Timothée Lacroix, and William El Sayed. 2024. Mixtral of Experts. *Preprint*, arXiv:2401.04088.

Tom Kocmi and Christian Federmann. 2023a. GEMBA-MQM: Detecting translation quality error spans with GPT-4. In *Proceedings of the Eighth Conference on Machine Translation*, pages 768–775, Singapore. Association for Computational Linguistics.

Tom Kocmi and Christian Federmann. 2023b. Large language models are state-of-the-art evaluators of translation quality. In *Proceedings of the 24th Annual Conference of the European Association for Machine Translation*, pages 193–203, Tampere, Finland. European Association for Machine Translation.

Guokun Lai, Zihang Dai, and Yiming Yang. 2020. Unsupervised Parallel Corpus Mining on Web Data.

Arle Richard Lommel, Aljoscha Burchardt, and Hans Uszkoreit. 2014. Multidimensional Quality Metrics: A Flexible System for Assessing Translation Quality. *Tradumàtica: tecnologies de la traducció*, 0:455–463.

Michael McCloskey and Neal J. Cohen. 1989. Catastrophic Interference in Connectionist Networks: The Sequential Learning Problem. volume 24, pages 109–165. Academic Press.

OpenAI. 2023. GPT-4 Technical Report. *arXive preprint*.

Shenbin Qian, Constantin Orasan, Felix Do Carmo, Qiuliang Li, and Diptesh Kanojia. 2023. Evaluation of Chinese-English machine translation of emotion-loaded microblog texts: A human annotated dataset for the quality assessment of emotion translation. In *Proceedings of the 24th Annual Conference of the European Association for Machine Translation*, pages 125–135, Tampere, Finland. European Association for Machine Translation.

Tharindu Ranasinghe, Constantin Orasan, and Ruslan Mitkov. 2020. TransQuest: Translation Quality Estimation with Cross-lingual Transformers. pages 5070–5081. International Committee on Computational Linguistics.

Ricardo Rei, Craig Stewart, Ana C Farinha, and Alon Lavie. 2020. COMET: A neural framework for MT evaluation. In *Proceedings of the 2020 Conference on Empirical Methods in Natural Language Processing (EMNLP)*, pages 2685–2702, Online. Association for Computational Linguistics.

Ricardo Rei, Marcos Treviso, Nuno M. Guerreiro, Chrysoula Zerva, Ana C Farinha, Christine Maroti, José G. C. de Souza, Taisiya Glushkova, Duarte Alves, Luisa Coheur, Alon Lavie, and André F. T. Martins. 2022. CometKiwi: IST-unbabel 2022 submission for the quality estimation shared task. In *Proceedings of the Seventh Conference on Machine Translation (WMT)*, pages 634–645, Abu Dhabi, United Arab Emirates (Hybrid). Association for Computational Linguistics.

Miguel Ruiz-Garcia. 2022. Model architecture can transform catastrophic forgetting into positive transfer. *Scientific Reports*, 12.

Hadeel Saadany, Constantin Orasan, Rocio Caro Quintana, Felix Do Carmo, and Leonardo Zilio. 2023. Analysing mistranslation of emotions in multilingual tweets by online MT tools. In *Proceedings of the 24th Annual Conference of the European Association for Machine Translation*, pages 275–284, Tampere, Finland. European Association for Machine Translation.

Matthew Snover, Bonnie Dorr, Rich Schwartz, Linnea Micciulla, and John Makhoul. 2006. A study of translation edit rate with targeted human annotation. In *Proceedings of the 7th Conference of the Association for Machine Translation in the Americas: Technical Papers*, pages 223–231, Cambridge, Massachusetts, USA. Association for Machine Translation in the Americas.

Charles Spearman. 1904. The proof and measurement of association between two things. *The American Journal of Psychology*, 15:72–101.

Lucia Specia, Frédéric Blain, Marina Fomicheva, Erick Fonseca, Vishrav Chaudhary, Francisco Guzmán, and André F. T. Martins. 2020. Findings of the WMT 2020 shared task on quality estimation. In *Proceedings of the Fifth Conference on Machine Translation*, pages 743–764, Online. Association for Computational Linguistics.

Lucia Specia, Frédéric Blain, Marina Fomicheva, Chrysoula Zerva, Zhenhao Li, Vishrav Chaudhary, and André F. T. Martins. 2021. Findings of the WMT 2021 shared task on quality estimation. In *Proceedings of the Sixth Conference on Machine Translation*, pages 684–725, Online. Association for Computational Linguistics.

Lucia Specia, Carolina Scarton, and Gustavo Henrique Paetzold. 2018. *Quality Estimation for Machine Translation*. Spinger, Cham, Germany.

Craig Stewart, Ricardo Rei, Catarina Farinha, and Alon Lavie. 2020. COMET - deploying a new state-of-the-art MT evaluation metric in production. In *Proceedings of the 14th Conference of the Association for Machine Translation in the Americas (Volume 2: User Track)*, pages 78–109, Virtual. Association for Machine Translation in the Americas.

Hugo Touvron, Louis Martin, Kevin Stone, Peter Albert, Amjad Almahairi, Yasmine Babaei, Nikolay Bashlykov, Soumya Batra, Prajjwal Bhargava, Shruti Bhosale, Dan Bikel, Lukas Blecher, Cristian Canton Ferrer, Moya Chen, Guillem Cucurull, David Esiobu, Jude Fernandes, Jeremy Fu, Wenyin Fu, Brian Fuller, Cynthia Gao, Vedanuj Goswami, Naman Goyal, Anthony Hartshorn, Saghar Hosseini, Rui Hou, Hakan Inan, Marcin Kardas, Viktor Kerkez, Madian Khabsa, Isabel Kloumann, Artem Korenev, Punit Singh Koura, Marie-Anne Lachaux, Thibaut Lavril, Jenya Lee, Diana Liskovich, Yinghai Lu, Yuning Mao, Xavier Martinet, Todor Mihaylov, Pushkar Mishra, Igor Molybog, Yixin Nie, Andrew Poulton, Jeremy Reizenstein, Rashi Rungta, Kalyan Saladi, Alan Schelten,

Ruan Silva, Eric Michael Smith, Ranjan Subramanian, Xiaoqing Ellen Tan, Binh Tang, Ross Taylor, Adina Williams, Jian Xiang Kuan, Puxin Xu, Zheng Yan, Iliyan Zarov, Yuchen Zhang, Angela Fan, Melanie Kambadur, Sharan Narang, Aurelien Rodriguez, Robert Stojnic, Sergey Edunov, and Thomas Scialom. 2023. Llama 2: Open foundation and fine-tuned chat models. *Preprint*, arXiv:2307.09288.

Shuo Wang, Zhaopeng Tu, Zhixing Tan, Wenxuan Wang, Maosong Sun, and Yang Liu. 2021. Language models are good translators. *arXiv preprint*.

Jingfeng Yang, Hongye Jin, Ruixiang Tang, Xiaotian Han, Qizhang Feng, Haoming Jiang, Shaochen Zhong, Bing Yin, and Xia Hu. 2024. Harnessing the Power of LLMs in Practice: A Survey on ChatGPT and Beyond. *ACM Trans. Knowl. Discov. Data*.

Chrysoula Zerva, Frédéric Blain, Ricardo Rei, Piyawat Lertvittayakumjorn, José G. C. de Souza, Steffen Eger, Diptesh Kanojia, Duarte Alves, Constantin Orăsan, Marina Fomicheva, André F. T. Martins, and Lucia Specia. 2022. Findings of the WMT 2022 shared task on quality estimation. In *Proceedings of the Seventh Conference on Machine Translation (WMT)*, pages 69–99, Abu Dhabi, United Arab Emirates (Hybrid). Association for Computational Linguistics.

Yaowei Zheng, Richong Zhang, Junhao Zhang, Yanhan Ye, Zheyan Luo, Zhangchi Feng, and Yongqiang Ma. 2024. LlamaFactory: Unified Efficient Fine-Tuning of 100+ Language Models. In *Proceedings of the 62nd Annual Meeting of the Association for Computational Linguistics (Volume 3: System Demonstrations)*, Bangkok, Thailand. Association for Computational Linguistics.

AI-Tutor: Interactive Learning of Ancient Knowledge from Low-Resource Languages

Siddhartha Dalal[1] **Rahul Aditya**[1] **Vethavikashini Chithrra Raghuram**[1]
Prahlad Koratamaddi[1]
[1]Columbia University
sd2803@columbia.edu

Abstract

Many low-resource languages, such as Prakrit, present significant linguistic complexities and have limited modern-day resources. These languages often have multiple derivatives; for example, Prakrit, a language in use by masses around 2500 years ago for 500 years, includes Pali and Gandhari, which encompass a vast body of Buddhist literature, as well as Ardhamagadhi, rich in Jain literature. Despite these challenges, these languages are invaluable for their historical, religious, and cultural insights needed by non-language experts and others.

To explore and understand the deep knowledge within these ancient texts for non-language experts, we propose a novel approach: translating multiple dialects of the parent language into a contemporary language and then enabling them to interact with the system in their native language, including English, Hindi, French and German, through a question-and-answer interface built on Large Language Models. We demonstrate the effectiveness of this novel AI-Tutor system by focusing on Ardhamagadhi and Pali.

1 Introduction

Much of the world's ancient cultural heritage is preserved in Low Resource Languages (LRLs) from the past. However, access to this knowledge is limited to a small group of linguistic scholars. For instance, Prakrit, an ancient language widely spoken in India about 2,500 years ago, flourished for approximately 500 years. Various forms of Prakrit, such as Ardhamagadhi, Pali and Gandhari, were used across different regions in India, Pakistan and Afghanistan. A significant portion of Buddhist and Jain historical, cultural, and religious texts are written in these languages. Unfortunately, experts in Prakrit are few in number.

To address the need for wider access to this vast ancient body of literature for non-linguistic experts, this paper argues that Neural Machine Translation (NMT) can unlock the knowledge contained within these texts. Given the archaic nature of the original language and the scarcity of scholars available to provide explanations, a question-and-answer format, powered by Large Language Models (LLMs), is essential for making this knowledge accessible to non-experts.

We demonstrate that these goals can be achieved by developing a Transformer-based Neural Machine Translation system and leveraging LLMs to facilitate interactions in a query-response format. This approach enables non-experts to engage with the content of ancient texts quickly and effectively. Specifically, we showcase this paradigm using Jain and Buddhist literature written in Ardhamagadhi and Pali, creating an AI-powered tutoring system that allows users to interact with an AI-Tutor in their own language, including English, Hindi, French, and German. The translation training data was sourced from original languages translated in Hindi and English.

2 Related Work

2.1 Low Resource NMT

Neural Machine Translation (NMT) has seen significant advancements, notably with the introduction of attention mechanisms, which allow models to selectively focus on relevant parts of the source sentence (Luong, 2015). As NMT evolved, researchers addressed challenges such as handling large vocabularies (Jean et al., 2014), translating rare words (Luong et al., 2014), and leveraging source-side

Proceedings of the Eleventh Workshop on Asian Translation (WAT 2024), pages 56–66
November 16, 2024 ©2024 Association for Computational Linguistics

monolingual data through self-learning and multi-task learning (Zhang and Zong, 2016). Efforts to optimize vocabulary sizes (Gowda and May, 2020) and tackle open-vocabulary challenges by encoding rare words as subword units (Sennrich, 2015) further improved translation quality. The development of massively multilingual systems marked a significant leap, enabling translation across over 100 languages (Aharoni et al., 2019).

However, despite these advances, NMT faces persistent challenges in low-resource settings, particularly for underrepresented languages like those in the Indic family. Low-resource Machine Translation (MT) struggles due to the scarcity of parallel corpora, which traditional NMT models heavily rely on. Transformer-based models have become prominent in addressing issues like word ordering and data sparsity in these settings (Vaswani, 2017). Noteworthy efforts in Indic MT have laid the groundwork for subsequent multilingual and pre-trained MT models (Philip et al., 2021; Ramesh et al., 2022; Kudugunta et al., 2019; Liu, 2020).

A key strategy to overcome low-resource challenges is **transfer learning and Fine-Tuning**, where a model trained on a high-resource language pair (parent model) is adapted to a low-resource pair (child model). This approach has shown significant improvements, particularly when the parent and child languages are linguistically similar (Zoph et al., 2016). Enhancements to transfer learning include **ensembling techniques** and **unknown word replacement**, which further boost translation quality (Zoph et al., 2016). Moreover, large multilingual and pre-trained models have been effective in leveraging linguistic similarities across languages, facilitating good-quality MT for low-resource languages (Dabre et al., 2020).

Recent work has also focused on translating extremely low-resource languages with minimal parallel and monolingual corpora (Maurya et al., 2023). Despite these advances, challenges remain, particularly in selecting the most effective parent language for transfer learning. As research continues, these innovations are expected to further bridge the gap between high- and low-resource languages, making NMT more accessible to diverse linguistic communities.

2.2 Multilingual RAG

Retrieval-Augmented Generation (RAG) (Lewis et al., 2020; Jiang et al., 2023; Gao et al., 2023) has emerged as a powerful method to enhance the factual accuracy and domain specificity of large language models by combining retrieval mechanisms with generative capabilities. While RAG has shown significant promise, much of the research has been centered around English-language applications.

Addressing this gap, (Ahmad, 2024) explores deploying RAG models in multilingual, multicultural corporate settings, focusing on strategies to mitigate challenges like hallucinations and optimize information delivery. Similarly in (Chirkova et al., 2024), the authors investigate mRAG models across 13 languages, emphasizing the need for task-specific prompt engineering and highlighting issues such as code-switching and fluency errors. These studies collectively advance the adaptation of RAG systems for diverse linguistic environments.

3 Datasets

To build and evaluate our models, we relied on several key datasets that encompass a diverse range of linguistic materials. These datasets were selected to ensure comprehensive coverage and accuracy in our training and evaluation processes. Below, we detail the datasets used, highlighting their sources and the challenges associated with obtaining and preparing the data:

1. **Pali Dataset**: The primary dataset for Pali training was sourced from Huggingface. It includes 148,813 sentences featuring Latinized transliteration and their corresponding English translations, provided by the Berkeley AI Research Lab.[1]

2. **Ardhamagadhi Dataset**: Training data for Ardhamagadhi posed greater challenges. The dataset comprises 44 Agams translated into Hindi by Muni Deepratnasagar, from which 10,113 parallel sentences were extracted.[2] Agams are the sacred texts of the

[1] Dataset available at: https://huggingface.co/buddhist-nlp.

[2] Translations by Muni Deepratnasagar available at: https://jainelibrary.org/.

Jain religion written in Ardhamagadhi and contain religious stories, art, literature, and poetry. These translations often included additional meanings, increasing the complexity of the neural machine translation (NMT) task.

3. **Ardhamagadhi Books**: In addition, five Ardhamagadhi books translated into Hindi and English by Professor V. K. Jain[3] were used. These books, originally provided in PDF format, were digitized using OCR technology developed by Mr. Kailash Mutha. Some scanned copies were obtained from an additional archive, yielding 910 high-quality samples.[4]

4. **11 Agams**: A subset of 11 Agams were available in English [5] which were processed by AI-Tutor directly without the translation pipeline.[6]

3.1 Data Preprocessing

To prepare the datasets for training, testing and fine-tuning, various sources of Prakrit sentences and their translations in Hindi and English were gathered and processed. The datasets comprised numerous code-mixed sentences in Hindi, English, and Prakrit, along with supplementary text such as verse explanations. Creating a clean and reliable corpus for training the neural machine translation (NMT) system required significant domain knowledge. This challenge was addressed through pattern recognition and efficient information retrieval methods. Despite these approaches, manual extraction, consultation with domain experts and verification were essential due to the complexities and exceptions inherent in the data, ensuring the accuracy and quality of the dataset.

4 Neural Machine Translation

4.1 NMT Base Model: Indictrans2

Indictrans2 (Gala et al., 2023) is a cutting-edge multilingual neural machine translation (NMT) model specifically designed for 22 current Indic languages. With its Transformer Encoder-Decoder architecture with multiple layers of self-attention and parallel processing, it can capture long-range dependencies in text, making it both effective and efficient for large-scale translation tasks for Indic lanaguages. Though many of languages covered by Indictrans2 are ultimately derived over thousands of years from Prakrit, it does not include Pali, Ardhamagadhi and other ancient Prakrit languages.

Indictrans2 is pre-trained on a vast multilingual corpus that includes text from various Indic languages paired with English and other target languages. A key strength of Indictrans2 is its ability to manage multiple languages simultaneously through a shared vocabulary and embeddings. By training on a diverse set of Indic languages, Indictrans2 learns cross-lingual representations, which are particularly beneficial for low-resource languages like Prakrit. In the context of Indic languages, pre-training on a multilingual corpus is especially advantageous due to the linguistic similarities and shared syntactic structures among these languages. For instance, many Indic languages share common grammatical features, such as subject-object-verb (SOV) word order and similar morphological patterns. Pali and Ardha-Magadhi are Middle Indo-Aryan languages that derive from Prakrit and are closely related to Sanskrit but are not directly descended from it. Sanskrit is a standardized dialect of Old Indo-Aryan. They all use variations of Devnagari script. Leveraging these linguistic similarities, we hypothesized that Prakrit's similarity to Sanskrit would enable us to initialize the encoder with pre-trained Sanskrit embeddings during fine-tuning.

4.1.1 Challenges and Limitations for using Indictrans2

Despite its impressive capabilities, Indictrans2 also faces certain challenges, particularly when dealing with very low-resource languages or dialects. For example, Prakrit, being an ancient and less standardized language, poses difficulties in terms of data availability and consistency. Additionally, cultural and contextual nuances that are specific to certain regions or time periods may not always be captured ac-

[3]Dravyasamgraha, Niyam Sara, Pravachansara, Samayasara, Panchastikay Sangraha. All from https://jainelibrary.org/.

[4]Additional scanned copies sourced from https://jainqq.org.

[5]Deepratnasagar Muni, https://jainelibrary.org/

[6]Jain era documents available at: https://jainelibrary.org/.

curately by the model.

4.2 Fine-tuning Approach

We utilized two variants of Indictrans2: Indic-Indic and Indic-En. The choice was driven by its ability to perform well in pairs of low-resource languages, making it suitable for translating Prakrit into Hindi and Prakrit into English. For fine-tuning with the 44 Agams dataset containing Prakrit-Hindi pairs, we employed the Indic-Indic variant, using Sanskrit embeddings as a means for transfer learning for Prakrit. Figure 1 illustrates the workflow for selecting variants of the pretrained Indictrans2 models used for finetuning on various datasets. The Indic-En variant was used for finetuning with the VK Jain dataset and the Pali-English dataset. Given the limited availability of Prakrit-English data, we employed a multistep fine-tuning process:

- The model was initially fine-tuned on the Pali-English dataset, utilizing Sanskrit embeddings for transfer learning, given the linguistic similarities between Pali and Sanskrit as both belong to the Prakrit family.

- In the next step, we use the resulting model checkpoint from the last step, now enriched with Pali-specific representations, and fine-tune on the VK Jain dataset to adapt it for Ardhamagadhi-English translation.

This progressive fine-tuning helped in gradually adapting the model to the nuances of Prakrit while maintaining the quality of English translations.

4.3 Results

Table 1 summarizes the experimental results across various datasets and fine-tuning approaches for the corresponding test splits. In all the experiments, we used train/dev/test split ratio of 80/10/10. Sample translations from the test sets of the Pali-English, VK Jain, and 44 Agams datasets are shown in Tables 2, 3, and 4, respectively. We achieved a strong BLEU score of 33.8 for Pali-to-English translations, benefiting from the large dataset. For Ardhamagadhi-to-English (BLEU score: 17.8) and Ardhamagadhi-to-Hindi (BLEU score: 14.9), the scores, although lower due to smaller datasets, are competitive with other low-resource languages such as Cherokee, where the BLEU score is approximately 14. (Zhang et al., 2020).

4.3.1 Pali-English Indic-En Pali-English

When translating Pali into English using the Pali-English dataset, the Indictrans2 model achieved a BLEU score of 33.8, chrF score of 54.7, and chrF2++ score of 52.6. This indicates strong performance and relatively high translation quality for the Pali-English language pair.

Table 2 shows a couple of sample translations on the Pali-English dataset.

4.3.2 Ardhamagadhi-Hindi Indic-Hin 44 Agams

When translating Ardhamagadhi into Hindi using the 44 Agams dataset, the fine-tuned Indictrans2 model achieved a BLEU score of 14.9, a chrF score of 34.3, and a chrF2++ score of 32.8. While these scores indicate modest performance, they are consistent with results seen in other low-resource languages, such as Cherokee. Despite the linguistic differences, the similar score range highlights the effectiveness of the model in handling low-resource languages, demonstrating its potential in such challenging translation tasks. (Zhang et al., 2020)

Table 3 shows sample translations for VK Jain dataset (Ardhamagadhi-English).

4.3.3 Ardhamagadhi-English Indic-En VK Jain

Fine-tuning on the VK Jain data set yielded a BLEU score of 17.8, a chrF score of 39.1 and a chrF2 ++ score of 37.2, underscoring the effectiveness of domain-specific data in improving translation quality. Notably, this performance was achieved despite the dataset's small size (approximately 900 lines), due to the robust pretraining of Indictrans2 and careful data preparation. Additionally, the use of a larger Pali-English dataset allowed the model to develop a coarse Ardhamagadhi embedding, taking advantage of the linguistic similarities between Ardhamagadhi and Pali. Finetuning the checkpoint of the Indic-En model trained

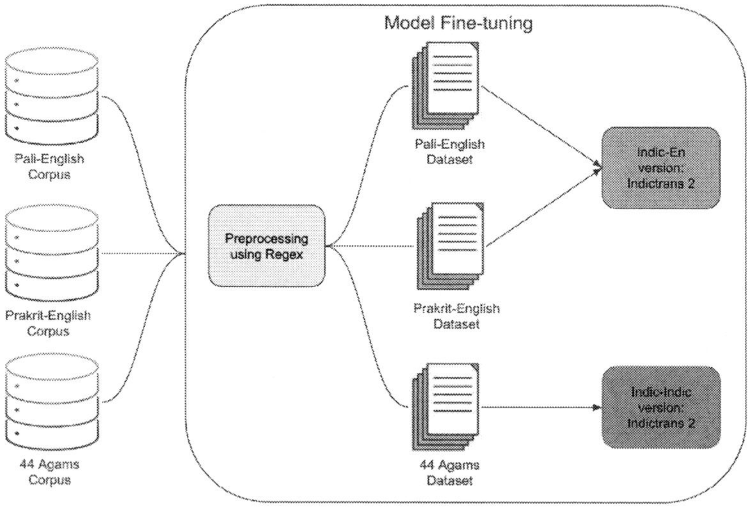

Figure 1: NMT system: Workflow showing parallel dataset extraction (preprocessing) and training two versions of Indictrans2 model during the Finetuning step depending on source and target language.

Source Lang.	**Target Lang.**	**Dataset**	**BLEU**	**chrF**	**chrF2++**
Pali	English	Pali-English	33.8	54.7	52.6
Ardhamagadhi	Hindi	44 Agams	14.9	34.3	32.8
Ardhamagadhi	English	VK Jain	17.8	39.1	37.2

Table 1: Results of Prakrit to English/Hindi Translations using Indictrans2 on corresponding test splits

Source: Pali	**Reference: English**	**Translation: English**
ऐवमेतेसं पञ्चन्नं खन्धानं समवाये आलोकनविलोकनं पञ्जायति।	Thus looking-straight-on-and-looking-away-from-the-front is seen in the combination of these five aggregates.	In this way looking straight on and looking away from the front is seen in the combination of these five aggregates.
अप्पका ते मनुस्सेसु, ये जना पारगामिनो;	Few among men are those who cross to the farther shore.	Few are those among men who cross to the further shore.

Table 2: Example translations from Pali to English using Indictrans2 on Pali-English dataset.

Pali-English dataset on the VK Jain dataset (Prakrit-English) led to BLEU score of 17.8.

Table 4 shows sample translations for 44 Agams dataset (Ardhamagadhi-Hindi).

We also observed a decrease in translation quality as the reference translation length increased. Since Indictrans2 has a maximum context length of 256 tokens, sentences longer than this were skipped during both fine-tuning and inference. The BLEU scores reported in the Results section reflect the subset of translations that fit within this 256-token context length. Similarly, for the 44 Agams dataset, almost 30% of sentences were longer than 256 tokens and had to be discarded.

[7]Obtained by Google Translate Hindi to English:`https://translate.google.com/?sl=hi&tl=en`

5 AI-Tutor System

The AI-Tutor System seamlessly combines the translation system with a multilingual query-response system. It is designed to facilitate multilingual interaction, allowing users to submit queries in English, Hindi, German, or French, and receive responses in their preferred language.

Source:Ardhamagadhi	Reference: English	Translation: English
जीवस्स जे गुणा केई णत्थि ते खलु परेसु दव्वेसु। तम्हा सम्मादिट्ठिस्स णत्थि रागो दु विसएसु ।।	The attributes of the soul do not exist in alien substances; therefore, the right believer has no attachment for the sense-objects.	The attributes of the soul do not exist in alien substances; therefore, the right believer has no attachment for the sense-objects.
ववहारणओ भासदि जीवो देहो य हवदि खलु ऍक्को ।	The empirical point of view indeed holds that the soul and the body are the same, however, from the transcendental point of view the soul and the body are never the same.	From the empirical point of view, the soul and the body are one.

Table 3: Example translations from Ardhamagadhi to English using Indictrans2 on VK Jain dataset.

Source: Ardhamagadhi	Reference: Hindi	Translation: Hindi
पणया वीरा महावीहिं ।	वीर पुरुष महापथ के प्रति प्रणत – अर्थात् समर्पित होते हैं । (Google Translate[7]: Brave men are devoted to the high path.)	वीर पुरुष महापथ के प्रति प्रणत-अर्थात् समर्पित होते हैं । (Google Translate: Brave men are devoted to the high path.)
परतित्थिय-गह-पह-नासगस्स तवतेयदित्तलेसस्स ।नाणुज्जोयस्स जए, भद्दं दमसंघसूरस्स ॥	एकान्तवादी, दुर्नयी परवादी रूप ग्रहाभा को निस्तेज करनेवाले, तप तेज से सदैव देदीप्यमान, सम्यग्ज्ञान से उजागर, उपशम – प्रधान संघ रूप सूर्य का कल्याण हो । (Google Translate: May the Sun of the Sangha form, who is a solitary person, who dims the aura of the enemy and is always shining with the brilliance of austerity, who is illuminated by right knowledge and who is the main one in the form of calmness, be blessed.)	एकान्तवादी, दुर्नयी परवादी रूप ग्रहाभा को निस्तेज करनेवाले, तप तेज से सदैव देदीप्यमान, सम्यग्ज्ञान से उजागर, निग्रह-संघ रूप सूर्य का कल्याण हो । (Google Translate: May the Sun, who is a man of solitary nature and who dims the aura of the world, who is always shining with the brilliance of austerity and who is illuminated by right knowledge and who is in the form of the union of restraint, prosper.)

Table 4: Example translations from Ardhamagadhi to Hindi on 44 Agams dataset.

5.1 Workflow

The workflow of the AI-Tutor System encompasses several key stages, beginning with query submission and ending with response delivery. Figure 2 demonstrates the pipeline. Initially, the user submits a query in one of the supported languages: English, Hindi, German, or French. For non-English queries, the system employs a combination of two translation systems: the fine-tuned IndicTrans2 model and the Argos Translate library[8] to translate the input into English, ensuring uniform processing of all queries.

Following translation, the system retrieves relevant content from a curated collection of Prakrit texts that have been translated into English. To facilitate efficient retrieval, embeddings of these texts are generated using the Sentence Transformers MiniLM model[9] from Hugging Face. This compact version of the Sentence Transformer model is optimized for efficiency while maintaining a good level of semantic accuracy. These embeddings

[8]https://github.com/argosopentech/argos-translate

[9]sentence-transformers/all-MiniLM-L6-v2

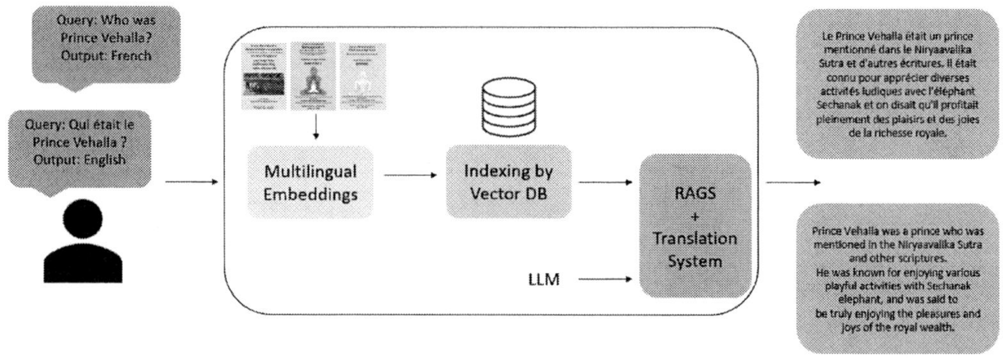

Figure 2: AI-Tutor System for Prakrit Texts: Workflow illustrating query processing, embedding generation, vector database indexing, and language-adaptive response generation using RAG and translation.

are then stored in a FAISS (Facebook AI Similarity Search) vector database, enabling rapid and accurate retrieval based on the query. For response generation, the system implements a Retrieval-Augmented Generation (RAG) architecture, utilizing the Llama 3 model[10] within the LangChain framework. The retrieved embeddings serve as crucial context, enabling the generation of coherent and contextually relevant responses.

In cases where the user requests a response in Hindi, German, or French, the system translates the generated English response back into the desired language using both IndicTrans2 and Argos Translate. Finally, the system delivers the response to the user in their chosen language. This comprehensive workflow ensures a seamless and robust experience, enabling users to interact with ancient Prakrit texts through a modern, multilingual interface. Table 5 displays an example query-response pair from the 44 agams dataset. More results are present in tables 6 and 7 in Appendix A showcase the example queries passed to the AI-Tutor System along with the responses for the three datasets. The result is a valuable tool that bridges linguistic gaps and facilitates research and education within the Indic context.

We evaluated the AI-Tutor's performance using GPT-4, focusing on faithfulness and relevancy. Both metrics scored 0.9 of 1.0 across 10 queries, indicating the AI-Tutor provides accurate and contextually relevant responses, proving its effectiveness as a learning tool.

[10]https://huggingface.co/meta-llama/Meta-Llama-3-8B

6 Conclusions and Future Work

We have developed AI-Tutor, a system designed to enable non-language experts to explore extensive literature in two low-resource languages (LRLs), Ardhamagadhi and Pali, by providing translations powered by Neural Machine Translation (NMT) and Retrieval-Augmented Generation (RAG). The limited availability of training data has been a significant challenge. Future efforts to generate synthetic data and incorporate additional training data from related languages, such as Gandhari, are expected to enhance translation quality. These languages, despite their differences, share structural, lineage, and historical similarities, which could be leveraged to improve the system's performance.

In future work, we plan to test our finetuning approach on Indictrans2 using embeddings from other Indic languages like Hindi, Gujarati, Tamil, and Telugu. These languages may be semantically closer to Ardhamagadhi than Sanskrit, potentially yielding better performance in translation tasks. Additionally, we aim to systematically compare these variations to gain deeper insights into how different embeddings influence translation quality.

7 Limitations

Translation work in this paper required converting pdf files to unicode text using OCR, which is not a full-proof process. We have used better system provided by Mr. Mutua to ameliorate it. Further, chunks longer than 256 tokens were not processed. We plan to deal with it by intelligent chunking of those unpro-

Query	Response			
	English	Hindi	French	German
How many types of devlok are there?	There are four types of devlok: Bhavanwasi, Vaanyaantar, Astrologer, and Wamanik.	देवलोक चार प्रकार का होता है: भवनवासी, वन्यान्तर, ज्योतिषी और वैमानिक।	Il existe quatre types de devlok : Bhavanwasi, Vaanyaantar, Astrologue et Wamanik.	Es gibt vier Arten von Devlok: Bhavanwasi, Vaanyaantar, Astrologe und Wamanik.

Table 5: Example Query from the 44 Agams Dataset passed to the AI-Tutor System along with the response in the supported languages: English, Hindi, French, and German.

cessed part. Further, the Ardhamagadhi translation quality needs be improved by acquiring more data and we are collaborating with linguist and domain experts to acquire more data. Finally, the LLM technology underlying the Query-Answer system can hallucinate. As the anti-hallucination technology evolves, we need to be able to incorporate better LLM models.

8 Ethics

We do not expect any negative social impact from our work. We sincerely hope that our work will further research for acquiring ancient historical, cultural and religious knowledge from LRL like Gandhari and other genres of Prarkrit languages used by millions two millenniums ago.

9 Acknowledgments

We gratefully acknowledge the domain expertise provided by Kailash Mutha, Dr. Jitendra Shah, and Pravin Shah. We also extend our sincere thanks to CUIT and Osman Kabir at Columbia University for their invaluable computing support.

References

Roee Aharoni, Melvin Johnson, and Orhan Firat. 2019. Massively multilingual neural machine translation. *arXiv preprint arXiv:1903.00089*.

Syed Rameel Ahmad. 2024. Enhancing multilingual information retrieval in mixed human resources environments: A rag model implementation for multicultural enterprise. *arXiv preprint arXiv:2401.01511*.

Nadezhda Chirkova, David Rau, Hervé Déjean, Thibault Formal, Stéphane Clinchant, and Vassilina Nikoulina. 2024. Retrieval-augmented generation in multilingual settings. *arXiv preprint arXiv:2407.01463*.

Raj Dabre, Chenhui Chu, and Anoop Kunchukuttan. 2020. A survey of multilingual neural machine translation. *ACM Computing Surveys (CSUR)*, 53(5):1–38.

Jay Gala, Pranjal A Chitale, Raghavan AK, Varun Gumma, Sumanth Doddapaneni, Aswanth Kumar, Janki Nawale, Anupama Sujatha, Ratish Puduppully, Vivek Raghavan, et al. 2023. Indictrans2: Towards high-quality and accessible machine translation models for all 22 scheduled indian languages. *arXiv preprint arXiv:2305.16307*.

Yunfan Gao, Yun Xiong, Xinyu Gao, Kangxiang Jia, Jinliu Pan, Yuxi Bi, Yi Dai, Jiawei Sun, and Haofen Wang. 2023. Retrieval-augmented generation for large language models: A survey. *arXiv preprint arXiv:2312.10997*.

Thamme Gowda and Jonathan May. 2020. Finding the optimal vocabulary size for neural machine translation. *arXiv preprint arXiv:2004.02334*.

Sébastien Jean, Kyunghyun Cho, Roland Memisevic, and Yoshua Bengio. 2014. On using very large target vocabulary for neural machine translation. *arXiv preprint arXiv:1412.2007*.

Zhengbao Jiang, Frank F Xu, Luyu Gao, Zhiqing Sun, Qian Liu, Jane Dwivedi-Yu, Yiming Yang, Jamie Callan, and Graham Neubig. 2023. Active retrieval augmented generation. *arXiv preprint arXiv:2305.06983*.

Sneha Reddy Kudugunta, Ankur Bapna, Isaac Caswell, Naveen Arivazhagan, and Orhan Firat. 2019. Investigating multilingual nmt representations at scale. *arXiv preprint arXiv:1909.02197*.

Patrick Lewis, Ethan Perez, Aleksandra Piktus, Fabio Petroni, Vladimir Karpukhin, Naman Goyal, Heinrich Küttler, Mike Lewis, Wen-tau Yih, Tim Rocktäschel, et al. 2020. Retrieval-augmented generation for knowledge-intensive nlp tasks. *Advances in Neural Information Processing Systems*, 33:9459–9474.

Y Liu. 2020. Multilingual denoising pre-training for neural machine translation. *arXiv preprint arXiv:2001.08210*.

Minh-Thang Luong. 2015. Effective approaches to attention-based neural machine translation. *arXiv preprint arXiv:1508.04025.*

Minh-Thang Luong, Ilya Sutskever, Quoc V Le, Oriol Vinyals, and Wojciech Zaremba. 2014. Addressing the rare word problem in neural machine translation. *arXiv preprint arXiv:1410.8206.*

Kaushal Kumar Maurya, Rahul Kejriwal, Maunendra Sankar Desarkar, and Anoop Kunchukuttan. 2023. Charspan: Utilizing lexical similarity to enable zero-shot machine translation for extremely low-resource languages. *arXiv preprint arXiv:2305.05214.*

Jerin Philip, Shashank Siripragada, Vinay P Namboodiri, and CV Jawahar. 2021. Revisiting low resource status of indian languages in machine translation. In *Proceedings of the 3rd ACM India Joint International Conference on Data Science & Management of Data (8th ACM IKDD CODS & 26th COMAD)*, pages 178–187.

Gowtham Ramesh, Sumanth Doddapaneni, Aravinth Bheemaraj, Mayank Jobanputra, Raghavan Ak, Ajitesh Sharma, Sujit Sahoo, Harshita Diddee, Divyanshu Kakwani, Navneet Kumar, et al. 2022. Samanantar: The largest publicly available parallel corpora collection for 11 indic languages. *Transactions of the Association for Computational Linguistics*, 10:145–162.

Rico Sennrich. 2015. Neural machine translation of rare words with subword units. *arXiv preprint arXiv:1508.07909.*

A Vaswani. 2017. Attention is all you need. *Advances in Neural Information Processing Systems.*

Jiajun Zhang and Chengqing Zong. 2016. Exploiting source-side monolingual data in neural machine translation. In *Proceedings of the 2016 conference on empirical methods in natural language processing*, pages 1535–1545.

Shiyue Zhang, Benjamin Frey, and Mohit Bansal. 2020. Chren: Cherokee-english machine translation for endangered language revitalization. *arXiv preprint arXiv:2010.04791.*

Barret Zoph, Deniz Yuret, Jonathan May, and Kevin Knight. 2016. Transfer learning for low-resource neural machine translation. *arXiv preprint arXiv:1604.02201.*

A RAG Examples

Tables 6 and 7 showcase the example queries passed to the AI-Tutor System along with the responses for the three datasets.

Query	Response			
	English	Hindi	French	German
Who is King Shrenik?	King Shrenik is the eldest son of King Prasenjit.	राजा श्रेणिक राजा प्रसेनजित के सबसे बड़े पुत्र थे।	Le roi Shrenik est le fils aîné du roi Prasenjit.	König Shrenik ist der älteste Sohn von König Prasenjit.
Describe the throne on which Shri Devi was sitting on	The throne on which Shri Devi was sitting on was named Shri in the Sudharma Sabha (divine assembly) of the Shri Avatansak Vimaan (celestial vehicle) in Saudharm Kalp (divine dimension).	सौधर्म कल्प (दिव्य आयाम) में श्री अवतंसक विमान (दिव्य वाहन) की सुधर्मा सभा में श्री देवी जिस सिंहासन पर बैठी थीं, उसका नाम श्री रखा गया।	Le trône sur lequel Shri Devi était assis était nommé Shri dans le Sudharma Sabha (assemblée divine) de Shri Avatansak Vimaan (véhicule céleste) dans Saudharm Kalp (dimension divine).	Der Thron, auf dem Shri Devi saSS, wurde in der Sudharma Sabha (göttliche Versammlung) von Shri Avatansak Vimaan (Himmelsfahrzeug) in Saudharm Kalp (göttliche Dimension) Shri genannt.
Who is Konika?	Konika is the name of a king in ancient India, specifically in the region of Magadha. He is known for his ambition and his actions towards his father, King Shrenika, and his younger brothers, Halla and Vihalla.	कोनिका प्राचीन भारत में, विशेष रूप से मगध क्षेत्र में एक राजा का नाम है। वह अपनी महत्वाकांक्षा और अपने पिता, राजा श्रेणिका और अपने छोटे भाइयों, हल्ला और विहल्ला के प्रति अपने कार्यों के लिए जाने जाते हैं।	Konika est le nom d'un roi de l'Inde ancienne, plus précisément de la région du Magadha. Il est connu pour son ambition et ses actions envers son père, le roi Shrenika, et ses jeunes frères, Halla et Vihalla.	Konika ist der Name eines Königs im alten Indien, insbesondere in der Region Magadha. Er ist bekannt für seinen Ehrgeiz und sein Verhalten gegenüber seinem Vater, König Shrenika, und seinen jüngeren Brüdern Halla und Vihalla.

Table 6: Example Queries from the 11 Agams Dataset passed to the AI-Tutor System along with the response in the supported languages: English, Hindi, French, and German.

Query	Response			
	English	Hindi	French	German
Explain the relationship between karma and the soul	The soul is the doer and enjoyer of karma, and the karma influences the soul's attributes and dispositions. The soul is not the creator of all attributes that are due to its association with karmic matter. The soul's attachment to external objects and its impure cognition are the causes of bondage.	आत्मा कर्म का कर्ता और भोक्ता है, और कर्म आत्मा के गुणों और स्वभाव को प्रभावित करता है। आत्मा उन सभी गुणों का निर्माता नहीं है जो कर्म पदार्थ के साथ उसके जुड़ाव के कारण हैं। आत्मा की बाहरी वस्तुओं के प्रति आसक्ति और उसकी अशुद्ध अनुभूति ही बंधन का कारण है।	L'âme est celle qui pratique et profite du karma, et le karma influence les attributs et les dispositions de l'âme. Lâme nest pas créatrice de tous les attributs dus à son association avec la matière karmique. L'attachement de l'âme aux objets extérieurs et sa cognition impure sont les causes de l'esclavage.	Die Seele ist der Handelnde und GenieSSer von Karma, und das Karma beeinflusst die Eigenschaften und Dispositionen der Seele. Die Seele ist nicht der Schöpfer aller Eigenschaften, die auf ihre Verbindung mit karmischer Materie zurückzuführen sind. Die Bindung der Seele an äuSSere Objekte und ihre unreine Wahrnehmung sind die Ursachen der Knechtschaft.
What are the unique features of the liberated soul?	The liberated soul is described as sense-independent, unparalleled, supreme, and free from obstruction. It is also said to be the real cause of liberation and is established in its own nature.	मुक्त आत्मा को इंद्रिय-स्वतंत्र, अद्वितीय, सर्वोच्च और बाधा से मुक्त बताया गया है। इसे मुक्ति का वास्तविक कारण भी कहा जाता है और यह अपने स्वरूप में स्थापित है।	L'âme libérée est décrite comme indépendante des sens, sans précédent, suprême et libre de toute obstruction. On dit aussi quelle est la véritable cause de la libération et quelle est établie dans sa propre nature.	Die befreite Seele wird als sinnesunabhängig, beispiellos, erhaben und frei von Hindernissen beschrieben. Es wird auch gesagt, dass es die wahre Ursache der Befreiung ist und in seiner eigenen Natur begründet ist.

Table 7: Example Queries from the V.K. Jain Dataset passed to the AI-Tutor System along with the response in the supported languages: English, Hindi, French, and German.

Author Index